Against Inclusiveness

JAMES KALB

Against Inclusiveness

How the Diversity Regime
is Flattening America and the West
and
What to Do About It

 Angelico Press

First published by Angelico Press, 2013
© James Kalb, 2013

For information, address:
Angelico Press, 4619 Slayden Rd., NE
Tacoma, WA 98422
www.angelicopress.com

978-1-62138-040-5 Paperback
978-1-62138-042-9 Cloth

Cover Design: Michael Schrauzer

CONTENTS

1

Introduction

Not long ago I published a book, *The Tyranny of Liberalism*,[1] that denounced the contemporary liberal state as tyrannical. One theme of the book was the destructiveness of inclusiveness as an ideal and program. I gave that theme some prominence, but it received next to no attention.

No one, it seemed, wanted to touch or even notice it. This is not surprising. To criticize inclusiveness means favoring exclusion. People find that frightening, and it suggests topics such as group differences that are imprudent to mention. Not long ago, the president of Harvard University and one of America's most eminent scientists both lost their jobs by making comments on sex and race that were rational, and relevant to important issues, but offensive to current sensibilities.[2] If that can happen to Lawrence Summers and James Watson, how can the rest of us feel secure?

Topics that are prudent for each of us to avoid individually may be disastrous to avoid as a society. Sex, religion, and ethnicity are aspects of human identity, because they relate to basic human connections. Without substantive debate, "inclusiveness"

1 Kalb, *The Tyranny of Liberalism: Understanding and Overcoming Administered Freedom, Inquisitorial Tolerance, and Equality by Command.*

2 At a high-level private meeting, Lawrence Summers commented that women feel the conflict between personal life and career more than men do, and men's aptitude for mathematics and science seems to vary more than women's, which suggests that more men have extremely high aptitude in those fields. Summers, "Remarks at NBER Conference on Diversifying the Science & Engineering Workforce." James Watson said in an interview that he is "inherently gloomy about the prospect of Africa," because "all our social policies are based on the fact that their intelligence is the same as ours—whereas all the testing says not really." Hunt-Grubbe, "The Elementary DNA of Dr Watson."

with regard to such matters has become an imperative that is transforming the whole of life. A realistic discussion of what it means to try to suppress those connections and negate their effect seems called for.

It is difficult to carry on such a discussion in a focused and intelligent way today. Highly-charged topics provoke misunderstanding, misrepresentation, and outrage, and it avoids trouble to accept established views. Also, such views correspond to established interests that do not want basic points called into question. Those who raise difficult issues are not likely to get a fair hearing and often lack the diplomatic skills needed for effective presentation of disfavored opinions.

Scope of the Argument

Under such circumstances, a general account of the arguments presented in this book may help sharpen the issues and focus attention on the views actually proposed. These arguments have limited scope and do not depend on contentious matters such as natural differences among races or the merits of particular cultures.[3] Instead, they deal with the role of cultural networks and distinctions of sex in social functioning and argue that such effects must be accepted and taken into account, if people are to live together harmoniously and productively.

The attempt to suppress or ignore such effects, I argue, is utopian in the way anarchy and communism are utopian. Sexual and cultural distinctions are too much intertwined with human life to be made irrelevant to how it works. Nor is such a situation something to regret. Every social order requires distinctions and exclusions, and everything human can be abused, so the issue is not whether making distinctions can cause problems, but whether there are human tendencies and functions that mean they must be allowed some effect. Discrimination of some sort is inevitable, and inclusiveness is itself part of a liberal political order that dis-

---

3 It is difficult to avoid such matters completely in a discussion of inclusiveness, and in a number of places I refer to controversies over them for the sake of illustration. The second paragraph of this chapter provides an example.

criminates based on wealth, bureaucratic position, political out-look, and formal certification.

The difference between the discriminations the liberal order allows and those it does not has little to do with any reasonable understanding of justice. At bottom, inclusiveness is merely one aspect of an attempt to turn social life into something like an industrial process in which human beings become components of a machine. To demand inclusiveness is to demand that these human components be distinguished only by reference to the demands of the machine and otherwise be treated as inter-changeable. This is why educational certification is acceptable as a distinction, while sex and cultural affiliation are not.

Such a conception is destructive, since human life is not mechanical. We conduct it through relationships that operate in a variety of ways corresponding to the diversity of human needs, functions, and concerns. Such relationships are not easily ratio-nalized and they always involve inequalities, since organization involves inclusion, exclusion, and hierarchy. The attempt, there-fore, to eradicate such inequalities suppresses basic functional aspects of social life and results from a view of social functioning that reflects a narrow and confused view of rationality. This dis-torted view of rationality is supported by basic confusions in thought characteristic of our time, as well as by particular class and institutional interests.

For the sake of freedom and human well-being, such attempts to remake social life should be abandoned in favor of a more *laissez-faire* attitude toward private discrimination at least. When there is abusive conduct, the response should not be one of abol-ishing distinctions that correspond to normal functions and con-cerns, such as distinctions of sex and particular culture, but should focus rather on specific situations. Such a proposal is, of course, radically at odds with what is now considered basic social moral-ity, so much so that its adoption would require basic changes in the philosophical and even religious understandings now established. I hope, if not to convince all readers it is right, at least to persuade some that there are good reasons for favoring it and that the assumptions behind the inclusivist regime are of doubtful solidity.

I will also argue for basic principles that I believe would lead to a more reasonable and functional social order. The understandings leading to inclusiveness are quite basic, which means that its principles inevitably touch on basic social, philosophical, and religious matters. Although restricted in its initial focus, this book is therefore far-ranging in its ultimate concerns and implications. I try to assume as little as possible in the analysis, however, so that even those who decline to follow my conclusions through on all points should find the discussion of interest.

The Inclusivist Regime

We hear a great deal about inclusiveness, but what we hear is more effusive than analytical. The result is confusion. A discussion of the topic should therefore start with basics: what inclusion is, what it is for, and what it does.

Definition

Inclusiveness expresses a demand for equal treatment. Liberals believe that the benefits of society should be equally available to all, to the extent consistent with the efficient operation of a liberal system based on technology, markets, and bureaucratic supervision and control. Furthermore, they consider it a basic responsibility of government and indeed everyone to make them so. The result is an ever more comprehensive campaign for equality with respect to certain dimensions of human identity.

Inclusiveness has become a central part of that campaign. It is an attempt to integrate groups that are defined in ways that are not relevant to the needs of the liberal system into all social activities at all levels. More specifically, it requires that persons of every race, ethnicity, religious background, sex, disability status, and sexual orientation participate equally in all major social activities, with nearly proportional presence and success established as the measure of equal opportunity for such participation.[4]

---

4 According to the Equal Employment Opportunity Coordinating Council,
A selection rate for any race, sex, or ethnic group which is less than four-fifths (4/5) (or eighty percent) of the rate for the group with the highest rate will generally be regarded by the Federal enforcement agencies as evidence of adverse impact while

As such, inclusiveness is one of a family of demands that differ slightly in emphasis and connotation. Inclusiveness itself seems to call for a universal warm embrace, while tolerance is more concerned with the dangers of hatred and persecution. Diversity and multiculturalism strike more expansive notes. Diversity celebrates the variety of the groups to be included and is supposed to bring strength, since each group is thought to contribute something special. Multiculturalism plays up the resulting mixture of cultural practices, which is thought to result in kaleidoscopic choice. In spite of such distinctions, all these expressions are defined so broadly that each implies all the others. It is not possible to be "tolerant" while opposing "diversity" or "inclusive" while opposing "multiculturalism." To accept one is to accept all, so that it would be natural, if repetitive, to speak of a "diverse, tolerant, inclusive, multicultural society."

Demands

A basic feature of inclusiveness that explains a great deal of its power is its religious quality. Inclusiveness presents a vision of unity in a world without outsiders and without borders, one in which there is no "they," but only "we." That vision is seen as an overriding goal, always to be striven for, though never quite achieved. Inclusiveness thus functions as a religion, and indeed as the established religion that determines how things must be discussed and what can be treated as real. Every view must align with it to be legitimate, and those who express doubts—the Watsons and Summerses—are treated as heretics.

Other religions that want to remain socially acceptable must assimilate to inclusiveness and become something other than

---

a greater than four-fifths rate will generally not be regarded by Federal enforcement agencies as evidence of adverse impact. —"Uniform Guidelines on Employee Selection Procedures (1978)."

A finding of adverse impact means that the employer is presumed to have discriminated and must prove he did not do so. Employers who want to avoid legal trouble and possible expensive litigation must therefore do their best to make the least successful group at least 80 percent as successful as the most successful group. For a discussion of the "disparate impact" rule in general, see Wax, "The Dead End of 'Disparate Impact'."

they were. Respectable Western Christianity has largely done so. In mainline churches, the Gospel is now said to be "radically inclusive" above all else.[5] In that setting, as in society at large, inclusiveness has become a principle of justification that covers a multitude of sins. Whatever his other qualities, anyone can become superior to the traditionally moral by invoking it. The latter are presumed guilty of bigotry, an unforgivable sin that requires perpetual confession and atonement that are never sufficient to restore the offender's moral standing.[6]

Basing social unity on a this-worldly religion carries with it certain dangers. If we are one because we are children of God, then it is His point of view that counts. Our unity transcends its visible signs, and we can understand it as real without insisting that everyone measure up in all visible respects.[7] When the vision is secularized, however, the demands of unity become more concrete and its realization more controllable, so the approach becomes more activist. The hard totalitarians of the last century adopted the most activist measures imaginable to bring about unity, up to and including extermination of those who did not fit in. Inclusiveness is much more subtle, but no less thorough. It allows people to be different, or so it says, but does not allow their differences to matter. Differences like purple hair are acceptable, because they have no functional significance. Differences like masculinity and femininity are not.

---

5 See 'Inclusivist Christianity,' pp. 135 ff. below.

6 See, generally, Gottfried, *Multiculturalism and the Politics of Guilt: Toward a Secular Theocracy.* It is worth noting that the meaning of "bigotry" has changed in response to the trends that have led to inclusiveness. The usual dictionary definition is still something like "obstinate or intolerant devotion to one's own opinions and prejudices." In fact, however, "bigotry" today is used to mean something like "regarding or treating the members of a group (such as a racial or ethnic group) with hatred and intolerance," with "hatred and intolerance" understood to include any judgment of a protected group that can be viewed as negative. See "Merriam-Webster.com." As a result, liberal or leftist beliefs cannot be called bigoted, regardless of how they are held or the attitude toward those who disagree.

7 "The kingdom of God cometh not with observation: Neither shall they say, Lo here! or, lo there! for, behold, the kingdom of God is within you." Luke 17:20–21.

To that end supporters of inclusiveness insist on suppressing the effects of distinctions that have traditionally ordered social life, but do not correspond to bureaucratic or commercial ways of doing things. This suppression is comprehensive: sex, culture, family, ethnicity, religion, and tradition are not a natural outgrowth of commerce or bureaucracy, so they must in effect be done away with. To this end grammar must be neutered, cultural boundaries abolished, family redefined to cover every possible living arrangement, ethnic festivals turned into festivals of inclusion, and traditional institutions diversified to the point of losing all definition. Distinctions of nationality must go as well, since they stand in the way of the comprehensive organization of all human things on the lines that are now considered uniquely rational. The American people must abolish itself as a people or complex of peoples defined by anything but inclusion, so that the goal of our national existence becomes self-transcendence through self-abolition. Mass third-world immigration becomes an almost metaphysical necessity, since without it traces of ethnic nationality would remain. Affirmative action must then be applied to force the resulting diversity into every nook and cranny of our national life. Anything less would be racist. Instead, people must sort themselves out by class, money, style, occupational level, and educational certification.[8]

Transvaluing Values

The abolition of traditional distinctions means the abolition of traditional standards. That does not mean anarchy, of course, it means new standards. So insistent are the new standards that even the military, which has urgent reason to emphasize effectiveness, group solidarity, and loyalty to country, now puts diversity and inclusiveness first. After the massacre of over a dozen soldiers by a Muslim officer whose professional failings and jihadist sympathies had been studiously ignored in the interests of diversity,

---

8 The requirement has spread beyond the American melting pot. The UN's special representative for migration, Peter Sutherland, has said that the EU should "do its best to undermine" the "homogeneity" of its member states. Wheeler, "EU States 'Must Be Multicultural'."

the Army Chief of Staff noted that, "as horrific as this tragedy was, if our diversity becomes a casualty, I think that's worse."[9]

To some extent, the new standards are based on the view that the old ones were bad, because they had to do with the non-commercial and non-bureaucratic arrangements of the old society. Reversing and violating those standards has therefore become a virtue. Central and marginal have changed places: Islam has become a religion of peace, homosexual couples stable and loving, blacks wise and spiritual, immigrants the true Americans. In contrast, Christianity is presented as a religion of war and aggression, Middle Americans as violent and irrational, Republicans as the Taliban, and traditional marriage as hateful, oppressive, divisive, and pathological. When women and minorities do well, they deserve the credit, when they do badly, white men deserve the blame. Any flaws in the groups promoted from the margin to the center are whitewashed, the more glaring the flaws the thicker the coating. AIDS has sanctified homosexuality, Muslim terrorism has made Islamophobia a horrendous sin, and black dysfunction has led to insistence on the hipness and nobility of blacks, the stupidity and tackiness of ordinary whites, and the sterility and oppressiveness of white society.

Anything less than the insistent reversal of the central and the marginal would allow traditional understandings of what is normal to continue. That result would be unthinkably at odds with the principle, which now counts as a social and religious absolute, that tolerance, diversity, and inclusion are unmixed goods. The point of celebrating Islam, homosexuality, or the public achievements of women is not to bring out the specific value of

---

9 "Nov. 8: Casey, Barbour, Rendell, Roundtable, Brokaw - Meet the Press | NBC News." It is worth noting that the Department of Defense report on the massacre declined to mention Islam or even the killer's obviously Muslim name. *Protecting the Force: Lessons from Fort Hood.* It is not just the Army that has made inclusiveness its supreme standard. According to a professor at the Naval Academy, both the Chief of Naval Operations and the Superintendent of the Academy have asserted that "diversity is the number one priority" there. Fleming, "The Cost of a Diverse Naval Academy." Not surprisingly, the professor was punished for his disclosures. Schmidt, "Investigators Say Naval Academy Punished Professor Who Criticized Affirmative Action."

those things—the less valuable they are in themselves, the better do they serve to undermine traditional hierarchies—but to provide a means of destroying the legitimate relevance of Christianity, the natural family, and masculine leadership to the social order by insisting on the superiority of their opposites. Nobody really cares about Sufi poetry. The point of "diversity" is not diversity, but rather simplifying society, subjecting it more thoroughly to governing elites, and getting rid of non-liberal principles of order.

Silencing Discussion

Most people find inclusiveness a bit silly at times, and there are complaints about some aspects of its implementation, but almost no one speaks openly against it as such. To oppose it, or even to fail to support it, is seen as an attack on the weak and marginalized. Such attacks are believed to be profoundly threatening to human well-being and also pervasive, since otherwise traditional social distinctions and the resulting need for inclusiveness as a special policy would never have arisen.

For that reason there has been little honest discussion of the nature and consequences of inclusiveness. Those in responsible positions say it is wonderful, and respectable people do not contest the point. Nobody can say just why inclusiveness is wonderful, and celebrations of diversity are notably lacking in enthusiasm, but questioning them would be awkward and inflammatory. It would also be a career killer, and career is everything among educated people today.

Among the populace there are still complaints, but in the absence of articulate leadership they remain at the level of resentful muttering. In any event, complaining is worse than useless. Opposition is treated as opposition to minority progress and thus proof of the need for stronger measures. It is considered *per se* oppressive. Indeed, criticism of inclusiveness makes it doubtful that all are equally welcome and so creates an atmosphere of exclusion that in itself violates the principle of nondiscrimination. The more serious and cogent the criticism, the greater the violation. Problems with diversity and inclusiveness must therefore be swept under the rug, with restrictions on discussion growing tighter, as development of the inclusiveness regime makes problems more evident.

Well into the '90s, well-known writers, notably Richard Epstein, Thomas Sowell, and Dinesh D'Souza, were able to publish books with major publishers asserting the rationality of at least some forms of discrimination.[10] Even less conventionally respectable writers, such as Jared Taylor, were able to publish books attacking basic assumptions of the regime with mainstream presses.[11] Today nothing similar seems possible. To all appearances, the publication of *The Bell Curve*,[12] which, however cautiously, brought the issue of race and genetics into play, brought relative freedom to an end by making evident the need for a stronger system of practical censorship. The Watson and Summers cases, and the difficulty established scholars have encountered getting their findings and conclusions in print,[13] demonstrate how powerful and effective such a system has become.[14]

10 Epstein, *Forbidden Grounds: The Case Against Employment Discrimination Laws*; Sowell, *Civil Rights: Rhetoric or Reality?*; D'Souza, *The End of Racism: Principles for a Multiracial Society.* Each was in a somewhat special situation. None is a white Christian. Epstein and Sowell are eminent scholars who base their views on economic analysis and statistics, while D'Souza attempted to put himself on the side of the angels by attacking those on his right as racists.

11 Taylor, *Paved with Good Intentions: The Failure of Race Relations in Contemporary America.*

12 Herrnstein and Murray, *The Bell Curve: Intelligence and Class Structure in American Life.*

13 As three engaged observers summarized the situation,

No mainstream publisher could be found for Phil Rushton's (1994) *Race, Evolution and Behaviour*—even the mail-order house Transaction pulped its 1999 abridgment of Rushton's book after threats from the US social science community; Wiley withdrew *The g Factor: General Intelligence and Its Implications* (Brand, 1996; 2001 edition available at http://www.douance.org/qi/brandtgf.htm) from UK bookshops; and Jensen found his own *The g Factor: the Science of Mental Ability* (1998) rejected by Wiley and several other mainstream publishers and given only mail-order publication.—Brand, Constales, and Kane, "Why Ignore the G Factor—Historical Considerations."

14 Acceptance of the existence of inborn racial differences actually dropped after publication of *The Bell Curve.* Guhname, "There Is No Silent but Sensible HBD Majority." Also see Derbyshire, "The Husks of Dead Theories."

What articulate criticism remains[15] mostly relates to minor aspects of inclusiveness or, occasionally, libertarian concerns—generally viewed as eccentric—about coerced association.[16] A few commentators continue to raise concerns about homosexuality or the violent tendencies of Islam.[17] Fewer mention cultural issues regarding immigration. Almost nobody except for a very few religious conservatives—the Southern Baptists are the major example—continues to object to the abolition of traditional sex roles. The concerns of such people are routinely treated in mainstream discussion as absurd, outdated, sectarian, or hateful. The Southern Baptists are typically viewed as comical, those worried about immigration as "nativist" or "racist,"[18] and those who accept the existence of racial differences as pariahs. Most recently, those who object to the full normalization of homosexuality have become targets of furious abuse and often physical threats.[19]

15 In the wake of Grutter v. Bollinger, 539 U.S. 306 (2003), a 5-4 decision of the United States Supreme Court that upheld the affirmative action admissions policy of the University of Michigan Law School, criticism of affirmative action basically vanished among mainstream conservatives.

16 See Block, *The Case for Discrimination*, for an example of libertarian concerns. Rand Paul recently got in trouble for noting that the Civil Rights Act of 1964 infringed on common-law property rights, but when pressed failed to articulate a good explanation of his position. See Thompson and Balz, "Rand Paul Comments About Civil Rights Stir Controversy."

17 Even *Time* magazine asked why the official report on the Fort Hood case never mentioned Islam or even the murderer's name. Thompson, "The Fort Hood Report: Why No Mention of Islam?"

18 Consider, for example, Gordon Brown's dismissal of a voter concerned about immigration as "bigoted" (Prince, "Gordon Brown Calls Campaigner 'Bigoted Woman'"), the claim by Linda Chavez, an established mainstream conservative columnist, that immigration restriction is simply a matter of fear and hatred of "the other" (Chavez, "Latino Fear and Loathing"), and the widespread view that it is *per se* racist for police to check immigration status in routine stops for other purposes. As time has passed views on the subject have grown far more extreme: as recently as 2000 the editorial position of *The New York Times* opposed amnesty for illegal immigrants. See "Hasty Call for Amnesty—New York Times."

19 See, e.g., Mullarkey, "Freedom of Speech—Unless You Annoy the Wrong People"; Messner, *The Price of Prop 8*.

Examples

The nature of inclusiveness can be illuminated by considering its application in particular settings.

The schools provide the clearest example, since it is there that the civil rights movement has won its greatest victories and run into its most notorious problems. Throughout the West, schools have been given the task of unifying religiously and demographically diversified populations and fitting them to the liberal regime. This goal is considered entirely within reach. Liberal modernity views differences as socially constructed and therefore removable through appropriate interventions. For that reason, diversity and inclusiveness have a comprehensive application to education, determining who gets in and what happens while they are there.[20] The specifics of subject matter are less important than the ethnic and sexual diversity of the participants and reading list. The indoctrination is direct, it never stops, and it has been remarkably successful. The more intelligent and highly educated people are today, the more they believe what they are supposed to believe.[21] The less intelligent absorb less of what they are told and retain more of their original way of thinking, but they are inarticulate and increasingly nonfunctional,[22] so they pose no threat to the regime as long as they are disarmed.

There are nonetheless knotty problems that are difficult to dispose of. While it is easy to find minority students and faculty, at

20 It is worth noting that there are a few partial holdouts, such as the California Institute of Technology, at which only 1 percent of the students are black, and New York City's gifted programs and elite high schools. "California Institute of Technology Overview"; Baker, "In One School, Students Are Divided by Gifted Label — and Race"; "Legal Clips >> NAACP's Federal Complaint Claims Entrance Exam for New York City's Elite Schools Is Racially Discriminatory." At Hunter College High School, in one recent year, the entering class was 3 percent black and 1 percent Hispanic. Otterman, "Diversity Debate Engulfs Hunter High in Manhattan."

21 See Guhname, "There Is No Silent but Sensible HBD Majority"; Guhname, "Are Attitudes Changing on IQ and Race?"; Guhname, "Political Moderation Shrinks as Years of Schooling Grow."

22 On the last point, see Murray, *Coming Apart: The State of White America,* 1960–2010.

least if acceptance standards are lowered and incentives offered, it is much harder to bring about ordinary levels of achievement. It has thus turned out to be extremely difficult to "close the gap" and achieve equality. Fundamental equality is presumed as an irrefutable given. Hence the disadvantaged cannot be blamed for their difficulties, and as a result the official reaction to failure is that whoever is in charge must be breaking the law by denying equal opportunity.[23]

Those in charge defend themselves against such accusations through grade inflation, slack or mindlessly rigid discipline, and non-stop happy talk. It would be invidious to distinguish well-behaved achievers from others, so grades and penalties have to go. Traditional standards, including standards of intellectual quality and substance, must be eliminated, because they are anti-inclusive, at least in their effects. Everyday judgment and discretion are discriminatory, since they are based on informal expectations that now count as stereotypical, so that good sense is dispensed with as well. The result is a new regime based on a conjunction of chaos, bribes, and insistence on an odd combination of absolute objectivity—"zero tolerance"—and unprincipled subjectivity, which has sometimes gone so far as to redefine the habits and attitudes of underperforming students as different "intelligences."[24]

From the standpoint of those in charge, the changes are not all bad. They multiply procedures and requirements that justify additional jobs while eliminating the need to achieve anything in particular. The more diversity and compliance with procedures become the goal, the less is it required of educators to produce anything. Parents and students can be bought off with assurances that standards are higher than ever and with promises of economic success through formal certification. The repeated discovery that gaps remain as they were can be met with astonishment and with assertions that more of the same is necessary to overcome institutionalized racial disadvantage.

---

23 See, e.g., Dillon, "Officials Step Up Enforcement of Rights Laws in Education"; Layton, "ACLU Alleges Michigan School District Violated Students' 'Right to Learn to Read'."

24 See Weissberg, "The Stealthy War on Smart Kids."

At times the relation between inclusiveness and personal advancement becomes crude enough to take on the quality of a racket. Academics can get promoted with little or no substantive accomplishment, if they play their (diversity) cards right, or else lose everything if they say the wrong thing.[25] Nonetheless, academic discussions show that at bottom inclusiveness is far from a racket. The belief that diversity should trump everything is quite genuine. It would not be nearly so useful as a ploy and system of patronage, if it were not felt so strongly as an imperative.

Employment is the other major prong of the campaign against discrimination and is also a rich source of examples. The effect of antidiscrimination laws is to require businesses to treat inclusiveness as part of their reason for being. To do otherwise would very likely inflict a hostile working environment on employees belonging to protected classes. A great many such employees would not hold the positions they do in the absence of affirmative action requirements. Thus, other employees will assume they do not belong where they are if those requirements are not treated as integral to the mission of the enterprise.[26]

So diversity must be given exaggerated importance, if it is to seem to make sense at all. Making a virtue of necessity, business leaders now insist that diversity and inclusiveness are good for business. That is no doubt true in some respects. Importing foreigners who are already skilled reduces wages and is easier than training Americans to do the job. More generally, mass immigration and increasing the numbers of women in formerly mascu-

25 When Nancy Hopkins complained about sex discrimination at MIT, she was put on a committee to investigate the situation and, not surprisingly, ended up with a rather generous settlement. Robert Birgeneau, the MIT dean who pushed her cause, was thereafter advanced to the chancellorship of the University of California. Taylor, "Why Feminist Careerists Neutered Larry Summers." When Lawrence Summers' reasonable and relevant, but impolitic, comment about women in science brought his career at Harvard to an end, it was Drew Gilpin Faust, head of the activist Radcliffe Institute for Advanced Study, who became president of the University. Mac Donald, "Harvard's Faustian Bargain."

26 Some lines of business are comparatively privileged. The demands and methods used for increasing the racial diversity of public service employees have been quite crude; not so in the case of Silicon Valley.

line settings decrease solidarity, multiply compliant workers, and increase the scarcity value of high-end managers and entrepreneurs. And it is of course beneficial from the point of view of business not to be sued or subjected to a campaign of defamation. It is doubtful, however, that benefits to society at large match the benefits to particular business interests. Feminism is at odds with family life, while competition from immigrants hurts American workers. Moreover, increases in ethnic diversity lead to inequalities, resentments, and disruption of social and cultural ties. And American society generally is injured by a regime of two-income professional couples at the top and fractured families subject to competition from a global labor market at the bottom.

Nor is inclusiveness always good for particular businesses. It means business decisions that willfully exclude or misinterpret important information and hiring people who for good reason would not otherwise be hired.[27] Quite generally, it introduces irrationality into the heart of business decision-making.[28] The subprime mortgage debacle, which began with bipartisan political insistence on increasing home ownership among financially shaky minorities, is one spectacular consequence.[29] On the other hand, the intangible benefits that are often claimed, such as creativity and cultural sensitivity, appear to be nonexistent.[30] Radical cultural diversity is at odds with the development and mastery of any particular culture and, therefore, with creativity, while rules against discrimination promote a one-size-fits-all approach that willfully ignores how culture works and intentionally suppresses its functioning.

27 For example, because of criminal records. Mandelbaum, "U.S. Push on Illegal Bias Against Hiring Those With Criminal Records"; "AL," "EEOC Files Suit Over Use of Credit and Criminal Histories in Hiring."

28 Schwartz, "The Clash of Moralities in the Program of Diversity."

29 See Morgenson and Rosner, *Reckless Endangerment: How Outsized Ambition, Greed, and Corruption Led to Economic Armageddon*; Sailer, "The Minority Mortgage Meltdown: More Evidence—But Our Elite Doesn't Want To Know"; Sailer, "Countrywide's Angelo Mozilo"; Sailer, "The Diversity Recession."

30 Guzzardi, "What Kind Of Waste Are They Managing?"; Rubenstein and staff, *Affirmative Action and the Economic Costs of "Diversity."* Also see 'Practical Benefits,' pp. 48 ff. below.

Meaning and Function

Inclusiveness and its related principles are novel standards. Their novelty makes it easy to fall prey to confusion regarding their meaning and implications. That is especially so, inasmuch as they are self-contradictory when taken literally. Toleration despises bigots, inclusiveness shuts out excluders, and diversity insists that we all line up to support it. Such features make it impossible to understand inclusiveness on its own terms and give rise to common right-wing complaints: why is it acceptable for the Congressional Black Caucus to shut out whites or Bill Gates to set up a special scholarship program for non-whites?

Such complaints are often cast as objections to liberal hypocrisy, but hypocrisy cannot be the real problem, when it is simply impossible for tolerance and inclusiveness to apply across the board. The real problem is that tolerance and inclusiveness make no sense as general standards. They establish a way of organizing society and so, in their very essence, they impose disciplines, make distinctions, and exclude possibilities. Most people are intolerant by official standards, so that the result of insisting on tolerance and inclusiveness is a general system of suppression. They are in fact principles that contradict themselves.

But, if the inclusivist project makes no sense on its own terms, what is really going on? A clue that may help answer the question, which has mostly been ignored except by idiosyncratic leftists, is that inclusiveness does not touch the forms of differential treatment associated with the ruling institutions of present-day society.[31] It is notable, but ironically not much noted, that the rise of inclusiveness has coincided with the rise of social inequality with regard to wealth, certified expertise, bureaucratic position, educa-

---

31 Compare Noam Chomsky's comment in Chomsky, *Understanding Power: The Indispensable Chomsky*, pp. 88–89:

> Over the long term, you can expect capitalism to be anti-racist—just because it's anti-human. And race is in fact a human characteristic—there's no reason why it should be a negative characteristic, but it is a human characteristic. So therefore identifications based on race interfere with the basic ideal that people should be available just as consumers and producers, interchangeable cogs who will purchase all the junk that's produced—that's their ultimate function, and any other properties they might have are kind of irrelevant, and usually a nuisance.

tional background, and other present-day markers of status and power.[32]

Inclusiveness is an aspect of an advanced liberal social order. Such a society denies the moral basis of power and inequality, because it takes equal freedom as its ultimate standard, so it needs to base itself on power and inequality that hide themselves. Rich and poor, PhDs and high school dropouts, CEOs and janitors, Supreme Court justices and ordinary voters, all have radically different powers, rewards, and opportunities. Inclusiveness insulates the privileges of the well-placed from criticism by giving them to women and minorities and so turning them into examples of equality. It licenses immensely privileged men like Colin Powell and Henry Louis Gates, Jr. to complain about their victimization, when they find their own treatment insufficiently special.[33] The message, which can hardly be missed, is that immense privileges are good and may even be insufficient, as long as PC standards apply. If there were no such privileges, how could a black man occupy the position Gates does? Inclusiveness, which has paved the way for PC yuppies and morally righteous international currency speculators, is at once the perfection and the death of equality.

32 On rising economic inequality in Western countries, see, e.g., *Income Inequality and Poverty Rising in Most OECD Countries*. Also see Paul Gottfried's discussion of the replacement of the economic left by the lifestyle left in Europe. Gottfried, *The Strange Death of Marxism: The European Left in the New Millenium*.

33 Horn, "Colin Powell Speaks About Racial Profiling and Gates." Also see 'Avoiding Hurtfulness,' pp. 45 ff. below.

2

Traditional Distinctions

Liberals pick and choose their discriminations. Financial, bureaucratic, and academic distinctions are acceptable, while natural and traditional ones are not. You can choose a Yale man over a Harvard man—the schools are a bit different, so their products may differ—but not a Yale man over a Yale woman. Engineers can earn more than janitors, and Chinese-Americans than the Scotch-Irish, but, if schools discipline blacks more than whites, that is a gap that must be closed.[1]

The idea, it seems, is that there is something odd and irrelevant about distinctions such as sex, family, kinship, culture, and religion that makes it wrong for them to have material consequences, unless the consequences disrupt the effect of such distinctions in general. People seem to think the principle is obvious, so it is never explained, but the idea seems to be that informal social hierarchies and the traditional patterns of conduct and belief that relate to them have no legitimate function. We should, it appears, carry on our lives exclusively through relationships that are either strictly private and idiosyncratic or contractual and bureaucratic.

---

1 See, e.g., Obama, "Executive Order—White House Initiative on Educational Excellence for African Americans," which noted that, "African Americans lack equal access to highly effective teachers and principals, safe schools, and challenging college-preparatory classes, and they disproportionately experience school discipline," and so established a government panel to promote "a positive school climate that does not rely on methods that result in disparate use of disciplinary tools." Also see Erbentraut and Resmovits, "Chicago Public School Students Face Racial Discipline Gap."

This book develops the implications of that view, examines its intellectual and institutional background, and compares it to views that are more tolerant of traditional distinctions. In this chapter I will attend to the last point and discuss traditional patterns, how they work, and why they are a necessary part of human life. In later chapters I will argue that the basic reason for wanting to extirpate those patterns is the belief that social order should be based simply and directly on the principle of maximum equal preference satisfaction. The issues this principle raises are basically technical. On such a view, the only legitimate social arrangements are technically rational ones such as bureaucracy, the market, and organized expertise. If other more opaque arrangements have an effect—if ethnicity affects success or young mothers are rarely found in demanding professional positions—something is disrupting the proper functioning of the system, and this is an injustice that must be rectified.

Traditions

Notwithstanding the strength of such technocratic views, man does not live by markets, regulations, and scholarly studies alone. There are basic aspects of life—birth, death, love, hate, family, friends, community, God, the Good, Beautiful, and True—that have to do with other things.

These aspects of life cannot be sealed off from the web of actions and relationships through which we carry on our activities in general. We are social beings and deal with fundamental concerns through settled patterns of life and thought shared with other people. Such patterns make up what is called culture. They are basic to the life of every individual and society and normally reflect a great deal of wisdom, if only because stupidity destroys itself. For this reason, they have considerable stability both within communities and in many respects across them.

These patterns and the communities that correspond to them define the networks through which we live. Most such networks are local and composed of people to whom we feel somehow related, by reference to whom we understand ourselves and our situation, and with whom we prefer to deal, because, when we do, we are in a setting we understand and trust. Family, friends, and colleagues are examples of networks that enable us to orient ourselves and understand our lives. The larger communities within which we live—church, neighborhood, profession, city, region, nation, civilization—provide other more extensive and enduring ones.

Such networks are basic to a life worth living. They make us part of a functioning web of habits, attitudes, loyalties, and beliefs that restrain, order, develop, enlighten, and refine our thoughts and actions. They give our lives definition by giving our actions purpose and order and our goals stability and coherence. Most of the things we do would seem pointless without them. Many people want to be CEO, but very few would bother to do the things a CEO does for the purely material benefits of the position enjoyed in hermit-like isolation. If considered apart from their social implications, the position and its material rewards would not seem worth the effort.

Human social networks grow out of practical needs, elective affinities, physical propinquity, and the common habits, understandings, memories, and loyalties that grow up over time and make complex social cooperation possible. They are at home in particular settings, and everyone is included in some and excluded from others. The resulting affiliations and exclusions are often affected by distinctions like parentage, class, and nationality that can be viewed as arbitrary. Nonetheless, such distinctions are not random impositions but rather a consequence of basic principles of connection, cohesion, and social functioning.

Such networks reflect human nature and other universal principles, but they do so in their own way, with content and contours shaped by history, local particularities, and what people find appropriate and satisfying. The marriage of man and woman provides an example. Sexual distinctions existed before the first fish crawled onto land, and definite settled connections between particular men and women have always been basic to social functioning. Some of the principles governing these connections have been stable; the need, for example, for them to be reliable and enduring. A society that fails to define, limit, and cultivate such connections in accordance with these principles has turned its back on human nature. This entails serious problems: relations between the sexes will lose form and functionality, people will not reproduce, children will be brought up badly, and men and women will be perpetually at odds with each other.

Nonetheless, the specifics have varied somewhat according to time, place, class, and type of society. The definition and functionality of the customs regarding married life therefore depend on boundaries and domains of applicability, that is to say, on line-drawing and exclusions. A mixed marriage can work, but it carries a special burden, and if too many marriages become too mixed, the institution of marriage will have difficulties for lack of definite expectations and standards.

Considerations of this kind make discrimination and exclusion necessary to any complex and well-developed way of life. Such a way of life cannot be fully inclusive as to lifestyle or religion, because it necessarily involves specific attitudes toward the good life and ultimate realities. Nor can it be so with regard to ethnicity, because it is affected by the ingrained habits, attitudes, and sense of common history and destiny that come into being when people live together for a long time. A truly diverse, inclusive, multicultural, and multi-faith society would have too few common habits, loyalties, and understandings to function except under mixed impulses of anarchy and tyranny. Some form of separation on ethnic, religious, and similar grounds is necessary for a society that realizes basic human goods.[2]

People object to this line of thought, because they want to equalize the benefits of society, but the benefits cannot be equal-

2 Something of the role of particular community in human life can be seen in Chesterton, "The Patriotic Idea," p. 19:

> Spiritually, then, we hold that a healthy man does not demand cosmopolitanism, and does not demand empire. He demands something which is more or less roughly represented by Nationalism. That is to say, he demands a particular relation to some homogeneous community of manageable and imaginable size, large enough to inspire his reverence by its hold on history, small enough to inspire his affection by its hold on himself. If we were gods planning a perfect planet, if we were poets inventing a Utopia, we should divide the world into communities of this unity and moderate size. It is, therefore, not true to say of us that a cosmopolitan humanity is a far-off ideal; it is not an ideal at all for us, but a nightmare.

ized without destroying them. They arise in their own way in idiosyncratic settings rather than through an overall scheme that can be endlessly reconfigured at will. The benefits of a party might be more fairly divided, if officials supervised it to make sure everyone in town had an equally good time, but it would not be much of a party. The example might seem irrelevant, since parties are notoriously easy to spoil, but the principle affects all pursuits. Man is social, and his pursuits are carried on in groups that develop a certain character and spirit of their own. Sportsmen have teams, believers gather in churches, artists and thinkers form schools, scholars have colleagues and colleges. Each activity and group does things its own way and does not normally do them as well if outsiders prescribe basic changes in conduct and membership for reasons extraneous to the activity itself.

Discriminations

Discrimination is simply dealing by preference with people of one sort rather than another. Universities prefer to hire PhDs for teaching positions, and that is discrimination. Most discriminations are less formal, as when a particular PhD is hired because of scholarly affiliations, personal recommendations, or how he impresses those who interview him. Discrimination need not mean absolute or even strong preference. Any mild preference that is sometimes strong enough to make a difference is sufficient. Such preferences can be based on any habit, belief, or sentiment, or on expectations of convenience, predictability, or efficiency.

There are usually sufficient grounds for them. We have a better impression of some people and some types of people than others in this connection or that. There are some we like to be with and others we like to avoid, and not everyone fits equally well into every arrangement of mutual cooperation. Most often, we deal with people by reference to their position in social networks. The network can be as informal as a circle of acquaintances or as formal as an institution or profession. It can be as limited as a study group or as comprehensive as ethnicity or religion. There is nothing odd about the resulting discriminations, since social networks are our usual way of connecting to people and doing things. To distinguish people by network is simply to accept the nature of human social functioning, since our position in networks guides our conduct and self-understanding and very often reflects other qualities as well.

As in most things, we should normally follow our own impressions, inclinations, and understandings.[3] If something seems natural to us, there is usually something to it, and, if not, experience will eventually set us straight. We must choose on some ground, so why not choose what we think we can understand, rely on, and feel at home with? That will usually mean sticking with what we know, since we know how established connections work, and they raise fewer issues. "Diversity is a challenge," and, rather than go out of network for some purpose unrelated to the matter at hand, people mostly do what comes naturally and apply habitual discriminations.

Fear and Hatred?

Proponents of inclusion often claim that discrimination based on non-liberal criteria has to do with irrational fear and hatred. No less unreasonably, they could make that claim about almost any choice or reason for choosing. People who join clubs for graduates of State U must hold alumni of other institutions in contempt. Those who take their coffee breaks at Joe's Diner must hate and fear Bob's Coffee Shop.

Such claims would be silly. They become no more sensible when transposed to considerations of sex, ethnicity, lifestyle, and so on. My innate and acquired tendencies, my manner of life, and the tastes, values, connections, loyalties, and expectations with which I grew up, determine how I am to deal with at least as much as my formal qualifications. There is no reason people should ignore the former but not the latter, even when the former bring sex, culture, and other innate or inherited connections into the picture.

---

3 See Gladwell, *Blink: The Power of Thinking Without Thinking*, although he dogmatically treats sex and ethnicity as simply irrelevant to accurate judgments.

Further, settled patterns mean discrimination. The non-technical and non-financial aspects of life are important, and people deal with them in patterned ways—in the case of sex, for example, through courtship and marriage. Such patterns, like all patterns, involve distinctions and classifications. We cannot demand that men and women ignore that they are men and women or that they have no attitudes regarding what that means. Nor is it wrong, in the conduct of life, to take into account common background, with its attendant memories, attitudes, loyalties, habits, and expectations. If we want good Chinese food, it makes sense to go to Chinatown and look for restaurants patronized by Chinese people. Something similar is true in our dealings with other patterns of behavior that vary by group. If we are attached or accustomed to particular habits of life, it makes sense to seek out a community in which that kind of life is valued.

Extreme or groundless dislike can play a role in the distinctions we draw, but among normal people it is hardly dominant.[4] The need to speak of hidden or unconscious racism shows as much. If racial hatred is invisible, why assume there is so much of it? Is not the insistent belief that it is so powerful itself hateful? Life is complicated. Most people just want to get on with it, and there are always a thousand explanations for how events sort out or why they follow certain patterns. It is not obvious why so many American diners and coffee shops are run by Greeks, but it would be silly and ill-natured to claim the reason must have to do with hatred.

Genuine hatred, fear, and contempt are hard to keep hidden. Many liberals hate, fear, and hold in contempt Republicans, fundamentalists, and white Southerners, not to mention Sarah Palin

---

4 For evidence it is ingroup love and not outgroup hate that leads to particularistic social solidarity, see Haidt, *The Righteous Mind: Why Good People Are Divided by Politics and Religion*, 234, 241–244; Yamagishi and Mifune, "Social Exchange and Solidarity"; De Dreu et al., "The Neuropeptide Oxytocin Regulates Parochial Altruism in Intergroup Conflict Among Humans." For the tendency of liberals to misunderstand the situation, see Graham, Nosek, and Haidt, "The Moral Stereotypes of Liberals and Conservatives."

and Mitt Romney, and they make no secret of their feelings.[5] Such attitudes should not shock us, at least up to a point. Some people are crabby, others annoying. Tastes differ, and people like to find scapegoats or have things their own way. So we have little trouble finding reasons to dislike each other.

The dislike is often mutual and sometimes justified, and circumstances are often complex, so there is no universal rule for what to do when people feel at odds. Sometimes they should try to moderate their aversions, sometimes they should change the conduct and connections that make them disliked, sometimes they should grin and bear it, and sometimes they should avoid those who make them unhappy. The last is often the most effective and sensible course. The old saying "absence makes the heart grow fonder" applies especially well in the case of people who rub us the wrong way.

Hatred can of course be destructive, but trying to eradicate it is like trying to eradicate selfishness or stupidity. Try to suppress it here and it pops up there. Suppress right-wing haters, and you will find that the campaign to do so is infested with left-wing haters. An obvious difficulty is that, when hatred is a real problem, people will not agree on who is at fault and what is to be done about it. The Nazis saw antisemitism as the solution and not the problem, and progressives rarely notice in themselves the hatred and contempt for non-progressives that has repeatedly led to the murder of millions of innocents.[6]

Artificial Divisions?

Another common view is that discrimination has to do with categories defined by arbitrary exclusions that advantage some at the expense of others. "White," for example, is thought to mean "not colored," where "colored" refers to those whose exclusion consti-

---

5 Survey data from the 2000 American National Election Study carried out by the Center for Political Studies at the University of Michigan indicates that a quarter of white respondents hate and fear fundamentalists as much as the most antisemitic 1 percent hate and fear Jews or the most antiblack 2.5 percent hate and fear blacks. Bolce and Maio, "Our Secularist Democratic Party."

6 See Panné et al., *The Black Book of Communism*.

tutes whites as privileged.[7] There are prominent academics who turn even sex into a social construction.[8]

Again, the best response is that ordinary people with a life to live and no special ax to grind know more about what distinctions make sense than academic entrepreneurs. The claim that traditional forms of identity are simply expressions of exclusion, like the claim that law is simply an expression of punishment or hierarchy an expression of domination and submission, may give some people a pleasing thrill of horror, but it reverses causality. In any normal case, the positive—what is constructive rather than constructed, what facilitates rather than oppresses—is more fundamental. The contrary view comes out of a belief that hatred and evil are more basic than good in human life. The belief is perverse, and, if true, there is not likely to be much that can be done about the situation.

It is true that human concepts and language include a great deal that is conventional. To distinguish cabbages and kings has an element of choice, and to speak of whites we must classify some as nonwhite. Nonetheless, people mostly attend to the specific problems they encounter in their own lives, and the things they find of interest are usually those that help them deal with them. We care about distinctions and identities, because they help us function by providing a definite setting with standards and connections that make possible stable and productive patterns of life. They tell us what we are, what other people and things are, the nature of our situation, and what actions make sense. How could we get along without them? The fact a distinction would not be made if people did not in fact make it does not mean it is arbitrary or even dispensable.

7 Sartre, *Anti-Semite and Jew,* with its claim that the Jew is at bottom the man others view as a Jew, is evidently a source of the theory.

8 Anne Fausto-Sterling claims that it is merely a "cultural conceit" to think that there are two sexes and calls labeling children as boys or girls a "social decision." Fausto-Sterling, "Sexing the Body." Judith Butler views sex distinctions as made up: "gender is a performance . . . the various acts of gender create the idea of gender, and without those acts, there would be no gender at all. Gender is, thus, a construction. . . ." Quoted in Felluga, "Introductory Guide to Critical Theory."

Social identities are not normally based on exclusion for the sake of excluding or exploiting. The family, for example, is a basic source of identity, and it is primarily defined by functions that demand a degree of mutual loyalty, understanding, and support that could hardly exist in an open-ended group. The boundaries and exclusions it imposes are a consequence of those functions and therefore secondary. Adam and Eve and the Swiss Family Robinson had no one to exclude, but they formed families that are like other families. The first pair may not have been conscious of themselves as a family, because there were no outsiders to provide contrast, but that did not change the nature of their connection.

Other traditional distinctions and exclusions work the same general way. Ethnicity matters, because people connect in networked clusters that help them deal with life by fostering common loyalties and patterns of habit and understanding. Those networks and clusters typically develop over time in settings provided by natural connections like physical propinquity and blood relationship. To discriminate and exclude based on such connections is to maintain a setting that allows established patterns of life to go forward. Ethnic neighborhoods arise not through artificial exclusion, but because people want to feel at home. The Japanese prefer to limit immigration not because they hate other people, but because they are attached to their own way of life and want to live with people who have been brought up in it and see it as part of what they are.

Once distinctions of identity are established, they can of course be used and abused like any human institution. Men sometimes act badly, and a scheme of identity that enables them to function effectively enhances their ability to do so. Such problems ought to be dealt with when they come up, but the solution for them is not to deprive people of their means of understanding their situation and acting in it.

Stereotypes

Discrimination involves stereotypes. The latter are social expectations as to what we do and are and are inevitable organizing principles of human life. To participate in a functioning pattern of social conduct is to accept stereotypes. If you want to be a host, husband, or historian, you act like one. If you refuse to play the part, people have the right to be annoyed.

To avoid stereotypes is to avoid particular expectations. To avoid sexist stereotypes, for example, is to expect nothing specific of men and women, and to fight sexism is to insist that everyone share your attitude. The justification for the insistence is not clear. Common sense tells us it is unrealistic, and it is impossible to make it stick. Requiring us to ignore similarities and differences that we unavoidably recognize as basic to human life is a recipe for cynicism, hypocrisy, irrationality, and fanaticism.

In any event, "avoiding stereotypes" does not avoid stereotypes, since we will have expectations of some sort in any event. Instead of stereotyping men and women, we will stereotype generic human beings, or maybe proles and professionals or liberals and bigots. The result will be a cruder fit between reality and the ways in which we deal with it than if we had continued to rely on the stereotypes of tradition and daily experience rather than those of ideology. Why would this be a good thing?

Discussions of stereotypes are often confused by a tendency to view them as simpleminded to the point of absurdity. Take, for example, the assertion that all Italians are excitable. Or else, at best, they may be seen as statistical generalizations regarding fairly simple qualities. The former view confuses stereotype with caricature, but the latter does point to one way stereotypes function. Groups differ on average in many respects, and group membership provides evidence regarding qualities that can be important.[9] If people see several young black men on one street in a seedy part of town and a small group of elderly Chinese women on another, most would feel safer going down the second street. The inference might, of course, be incorrect. The elderly women might be suicide cultists about to blow themselves up, the young men pious monks devoted to poverty and good works with robes that look from a distance like hoodies and baggy pants. That information, if available, would be far more

9 See Jussim, *Social Perception and Social Reality*; Jussim, McCauley, and Lee, *Stereotype Accuracy: Toward Appreciating Group Differences*.

useful than general statistical tendencies. On the other hand, particular indications must be interpreted by reference to their setting, and Bayes' Theorem tells us that group membership continues to provide evidence regarding the real situation regardless of how much other information is available.[10] If all we knew about each group apart from race, sex, and age was that some of their number suffered from drug-impaired judgment, it might be reasonable to interpret that information differently in each case.

More often, however, stereotypes relate less to simple characteristics that can easily be reduced to statistics than to complex and often subtle patterns that have to do with social roles. Doctors, lawyers, and Indian chiefs differ and should be treated differently, but not because of statistical tendencies with regard to simple human qualities. They differ by role. How people act depends on a complex of habits, attitudes, expectations, and reactions. They pick up that complex mostly from those around them, so that it varies from group to group and from position to position within a group. The result is that even people who are similar in many ways may act very differently in this setting or that.

These differences relate to functional patterns, so they are normally somewhat predictable. We expect dealing with the French to be different from dealing with the Dutch, even though the two have lived side by side for many centuries and are not strikingly different on most measures. People try to capture some of these differences by speaking of the Cartesian French and the stolid Dutch, but the distinctions are subtle and often ambiguous and cannot be applied in a mechanical way. Similarly, men and women are notoriously different, but the exact differences can be difficult to pin down. The situation is a fertile field for wit and paradox. Whatever men and women say about each other, and however true it may be, it often seems that the opposite is also true in some sense.

---

10   Miller, "The Relevance of Group Membership for Personnel Selection: A Demonstration Using Bayes' Theorem."

Basic Distinctions

The subtlety and complexity of human distinctions are part of the subtlety and complexity of human life. Social settings are always complicated, and each differs somewhat from all the others. To live competently as a human being is to deal with the complications, differences, and ambiguities in a way that makes sense. Part of that process is taking particularities of group functioning into account. What works depends on who is involved, and the "who" has a group component. All-star teams never measure up. In many connections, cohesion, complementary qualities, and common understandings are more important than individual talent and skill. When the point is the enhancement of functionality, judging us "as individuals" is often an error.

Sex

In particular, a group of men, a group of women, and a mixed group behave differently. All societies have recognized and made use of the differences, so that sex has always and everywhere been basic to social organization. Tolerance for natural inclinations, respect for the universal consensus of mankind, and consideration of the damage done to family stability and human well-being by increasingly ill-defined sex roles suggest that we should accept and cooperate with sexual differences and their effect on attitudes and actions. But if this is done, men and women will be brought up differently and, quite apart from natural differences, it will be no more irrational to discriminate between them in employment and other connections than to discriminate between people who differ in formal education.

Ethnicity

Ethnicity also affects social functioning. An ethnic culture is a system of social cooperation, a structure of habits, standards, attitudes, and roles that has grown up among people who have lived and worked together for many generations. Different groups do things differently, so these systems differ. That is why those who share ethnic culture usually find it more pleasant and productive to associate together. It is easier to be productive with people who have similar reactions and understandings of how things should work.

"Cultural sensitivity" is necessary, when we deal with those from other backgrounds, so much so that ethnic diversity is a major challenge leading to numerous issues that require special training and procedures to deal with. Not every employer wants to multiply major challenges, and there is no general obligation to do so. It is as reasonable for one who would rather have some things just work without special effort to seek out a niche in the market for people to hire, that is to say, to engage in employment discrimination, as to look for a niche in the market for products to sell.

For example, Japanese and Irish people have been brought up since childhood to function in different settings. It is legitimate to take that background into account in hiring and promotion. No one would be upset if Pat Clancy goes to work for Donovan's Pub rather than Suzuki's Sake House, because he thinks he will fit in better there. Conversely, if Kenzo Ohara gets hired at someone's Tokyo office instead of Kenneth O'Hara, because people expect fewer issues, that is rational, even if the expectation is based on ethnic background.

Religion

A religion is a basic understanding of man and the world. As such, it is obviously relevant to human cooperation and thus to our choice of those with whom we establish connections. In other words, it is clearly rational to use it as a basis for discrimination with regard to important relationships like employment. The mystery is how anyone could ever have thought otherwise. It is true that some people adhere only nominally to what they call their religion, so that it has no significant effect on anything they do, but what grounds are there to insist on this attitude as a required norm?

Formal and Informal Institutions

Social networks become concrete in institutions. Institutions always involve distinctions and therefore discriminations of some sort. They differ greatly in degree of formality. Good manners and tailgating at football games are institutions, and so are the federal income tax and the Lisp computer language. In general, the formal depends on the informal. Statutory law is formal, social attitudes informal, and it depends on the latter how the former is understood and applied and, indeed, whether it carries any weight at all.

The priority of informal institutions was more obvious in earlier times. In traditional European monarchies, for example, position in the government was often a direct matter of personal connection to the king. You became king by having the king as your father, and a "count" was one of the king's companions or *comites*. This informality allowed men to get by with very little formal training or bureaucracy, relying instead on everyday expectations and networks of informal relationships. Under such circumstances, it went without saying that particular background and connections were basic to what a man was and his position in the world. An animus against "discrimination" would have made no sense. It would have been like an animus against recognizing differences in wealth or rank in a commercial or military society.

This attitude persisted to some extent until quite recently. Not long ago it was common sense to distinguish a Connecticut Yankee from a Southern black, to expect different things from each, and to act accordingly. Today such a distinction would be considered outrageous. Instead, people think it reasonable to distinguish a Harvard from a West Point graduate. Technology is considered the rational way to deal with men as well as things, so that people base their assumptions on how others have been processed. Harvard turns out one kind of person, West Point another, so the two should be treated differently.

Such an attitude reflects a world in which formal expertise, bureaucratic regulation, and global markets are considered the sole rational means of social organization. In such a world, people come to view traditional informal institutions and expectations as irrational and therefore illegitimate. That view makes little sense. Not everything can be formalized. The universal importance of personal contacts in hiring, not to mention the possibility of a rule-book slowdown,[11] shows as much.

Even today, informal connections, understandings, and arrangements, and the roles, exclusions, and discriminations on which they depend, are fundamental to social life. If they were not, imposition of more regulation and bureaucracy would be a reliable way to improve quality and efficiency. Intentionally to disrupt informal arrangements simply as such and to try to keep them from affecting social life because of their supposed irrationality and injustice is therefore to strike at the root of social functioning. In this, as in other respects, liberalism is radically antihuman, because it rejects basic features of human life. It is able to exist only by virtue of what it rejects.

11 A form of job action in which workers slow activity to a crawl by following written procedures literally.

3

Antidiscrimination
& Inclusiveness

We have seen that prejudice and discrimination are necessary and useful in the way other basic social principles, such as property rights and the coercive power of government, are necessary and useful. Such principles have often lent themselves to abuse and are subject to limitation as part of a larger scheme of human life, but they are basic to social functioning, and we cannot do without them.

Discrimination Prohibited

Here are some examples of prejudice and discrimination:

- Sometimes expecting different things of men and women and treating them accordingly.

- Believing that the differences are complementary and adapted to enduring unions that are basic to everyday life, social order, and the continuation of the species.

- Giving specific legal recognition and support to such unions.

- Believing that different peoples—Westerners, South Asians, Jews, Irishmen, Fukienese peasants—have different qualities and ways of doing things.

- Feeling more or less attracted to one group or another, feeling most at home with one's own group, and feeling at times that there are groups one would rather avoid.

- Taking religious, ethnic, and other communal ties into account in choosing basic affiliations like whom to marry, where to live, and whom to work with.

Until very recently, such things have always counted as ordinary good sense, so much so that they hardly ever surfaced as issues. "Sexist" and "homophobic" are notoriously post-'60s coinages. Even "racist" is a fairly new word,[1] its extremely broad application still more so, and until recently "bigot" had to do with narrowness and obstinacy in matters of opinion rather than a tendency to make distinctions in matters like race. Nonetheless, distinctions such as sex, religion, and inherited community that have always ordered human life are now treated as moral horrors. Ordinary examples of discrimination like the ones mentioned must be extirpated.[2] Social arrangements that matter must be purged of any trace of them and based instead on neutral bureaucratic and market criteria. We are allowed to take natural and traditional ties into account only in personal settings that grow ever more narrow, or in order to cancel out effects such ties might otherwise have.[3]

Nondiscrimination claims to appeal to simple reason and justice, but it imposes demands that are sometimes more than a little odd:

- Military experience can count in employment decisions and the like, but not the experience of being raised a man rather than a woman, or even the consequences of hundreds of millions of years of sexual dimorphism.

- Employers may distinguish between college graduates and

---

1 Its first known use is from 1933. "Merriam-Webster.com."

2 As the French Gayssot Act states, "any discrimination founded on membership or non-membership of an ethnic group, a nation, a race or a religion is prohibited."

3 The latter exception means that people are encouraged to assert their racial, religious, and sexual identities, if they are out of the ordinary, so that the assertion destabilizes arrangements like inherited culture and the standards and conventions that support family life, which rely on schemes of identity traditionally dominant.

dropouts or even Yale and Harvard graduates, but not May-flower descendants and Mexican immigrants, except to the extent that immigrants need a boost to help them overcome disadvantages.

• Habits, attitudes, and loyalties can matter, but only if they have no connection to cultural community. You can insist that new employees attend diversity training and take into account their commitment to multiculturalism, but not consider whether they are churchgoers. The latter approach might get you better employees who work more happily together, but it is illegal.

• Schools can exclude people from teaching irrespective of individual merit if they have not taken useless education courses, but it is a crushing objection to sex discrimination in the military that some women are bigger, stronger, braver, or more stoic than some men.

• An employer can demand a bachelor's degree for non-technical entry-level positions, but not (in general) look at IQ or criminal records in deciding who to hire. Some minorities come out badly on the latter criteria, and they are less amenable than educational certifications to affirmative action fudges. The result is that they cannot be used unless shown to be job-related by standards that are usually impractical to satisfy beyond risk of lawsuits.

• In more and more settings it is illegal to treat sex as relevant to family relationships. In some places it must be ignored even in situations like adoption that involve utterly powerless parties with no choice in the matter.

It is said we are free to make whatever distinctions we want in private settings. That freedom cannot amount to much, since public and private are intertwined. Truth and morality are essentially public standards, so what is morally compulsory in public life can hardly fail to transform what is thought appropriate in human relations generally. As Chai Feldblum, a law professor and member of the federal Equal Employment Opportunity Commission, points out, homosexual equality, like racial equality, requires social intolerance of private beliefs, including religious beliefs, that may negatively affect it.[4]

Such a situation makes no sense, but people do not know how to dispute it. The result is that everyone who participates in public life today, including any minimally active citizen, and anyone with a responsible position in an organization of any size, must either lose credit as an opponent of human decency or claim devotion to a sacred cause that makes no sense and disrupts normal social functioning. Almost everyone goes along with that expectation, and no one, except a few liberals looking back on the horrors of the past and celebrating the triumph of their cause, notices how radical it is.

To accept as mainstream a principle as intrinsically radical as nondiscrimination is to accept permanent revolution as mainstream and the basis of social order. Gerald Ford set the gold standard for middle-American moderately conservative leadership, and he supported government benefits for same-sex couples. At the time of his funeral, many thought his social views worth emphasizing for that reason.[5] It appears that no living former president would dispute those views. All take it for granted that sex and social order should be irrelevant to each other, so that there is no legitimate reason to treat two men differently from a man and a woman in any connection.

An obvious consequence is the abolition of the family as a natural institution with distinct features that make it basic to the social order. To accept this consequence is to set forth on uncharted and obviously perilous waters. But how could eminent public men like the two former presidents propose anything different? There is no good way to reject the gay agenda, unless you reject the feminist agenda, and no good way to do that, unless

---

4 Feldblum, "Moral Conflict and Liberty: Gay Rights and Religion."

5 Jimmy Carter, for example, pointed out in his eulogy that he and Ford agreed that, "Christians should not be divided over seemingly important, but tangential issues, including sexual preferences and the role of women in the church," where "not be divided" evidently means "united in accepting the liberal position." Carter, "Former U.S. President Jimmy Carter's Remarks at the Funeral Service for President Gerald R. Ford."

you think "stereotypes and discrimination," that is to say, the acceptance of the relevance of traditional components of personal and social identity to the conduct of daily life, are acceptable. And from any remotely mainstream point of view, they are not.

On to Inclusiveness

Radical though it is, the nondiscrimination standard has been supplemented by the still more demanding ideal of inclusiveness. To a large extent, the former has been merged into the latter, so that the inclusiveness standard is now primary. This standard tells us that disproportionate results are intolerable simply as such. We must "celebrate diversity" and do what we can to increase it in all settings, with the goal being proportionate representation of all groups not specifically defined by reference to the needs of commercial and bureaucratic institutions. The alternative is thought to be denial of the humanity of those excluded.

Inclusiveness does not have quite the absolute authority that nondiscrimination does, if only because its demands are much more open-ended and therefore less well-defined, but few are willing to oppose it. Almost all educated people accept it as a necessary aspiration. It seems not quite right—incomplete and even somewhat antisocial—when an institution or activity is too white or too male.[6] If NASCAR or the Tea Parties are heavily white, it is a big problem for them, since it demonstrates a pattern of practical exclusion that is evidently accepted by those involved and therefore as good as intentional.[7]

---

6 Consider, for example, the efforts by English authorities to increase non-white participation in fishing. Partner, "Is Angling a Racist Sport?"

7 It is even a problem if Mitt Romney is too polite and dresses too neatly, since that makes him "too white." Siegel, "What's Race Got to Do With It?" On the other hand, the view of the Tea Parties as a white movement seems exaggerated. Saad, *Tea Partiers Are Fairly Mainstream in Their Demographics*. All such problems recede to the vanishing point, if the person or group is not otherwise under suspicion. Classical music fans are not considered racist, even though they include few blacks and Hispanics, and Joe Biden could call Barack Obama "the first mainstream African-American who is articulate and bright and clean and a nice-looking guy" without serious consequences.

But why is this the attitude? People treat inclusiveness as beyond discussion. They present it as modern, exciting, creative, caring, strengthening, and whatnot else. This, of course, is happy talk—sentimental, gratuitous, and obviously made up. The real basis for it must be inferred from the situation as a whole. Here are some considerations that seem relevant:

• Inclusiveness provides a way to make radical principles more palatable to the majority by changing the focus from the guilt of discrimination to the excitement of diversity.[8]

• It makes the civil rights laws easier to apply, since it makes proof of specific discrimination unnecessary. Claims of actual discrimination are still made and provoke righteous outrage, but there is no point rebutting them. To rebut them is to say that exclusion is acceptable; women and disadvantaged minorities should indeed be treated fairly, but they have a place and it is fair for them to stay in it.

• It tells us that diversity is always good and so obviates defenses of discrimination based on the rationality of taking differences into account. It thus makes it possible to recognize obvious cultural or biological differences to the extent needed to accommodate them without raising the awkward possibility that they might sometimes cause problems.

• It makes it easier to extend affirmative action to immigrants and others who are harder than American blacks to portray as victims of longstanding injustice. When expanded, moreover, to the celebration of diversity, it eliminates objections to continual mass immigration from everywhere.

A more basic reason for the move to inclusiveness, however, is the fundamental radicalism of the antidiscrimination principle. Progress progresses, and inclusiveness is a natural continuation of the civil rights movement. The original goals of that movement, after all, included integration as well as desegregation. The legal abolition of overt discrimination left most things as they were. That is to say, inequality and separation refused to go away. This

---

8 See Sowell, *Civil Rights: Rhetoric or Reality?*

situation could not be attributed to actual differences or legitimate attitudes and practices, so it had to be blamed on hidden bigotries and ever more subtle structural injustices that required stronger and stronger measures to search out and destroy. The war against discrimination, therefore, soon led to measures such as quotas, sensitivity training, the bowdlerization of language, the redefinition of merit, and the compulsory celebration of diversity.

The problem is that we are sexual and cultural beings, so that sexual and cultural distinctions are basic to how we connect and function. But to allow either to affect human relations and social functioning means discrimination. It follows that eliminating discrimination requires all practices and institutions to be transformed from top to bottom in unprecedented and indeed impossible ways. There are always new fronts on which to prosecute a battle that can never be won against an evil that is intrinsic to social life. Racism and sexism are everywhere, and, even where they are irrelevant, complaints must be taken seriously. Members of protected classes will feel rejected, if they are told their complaints have no merit, and the result is that we must accept them at face value. In the most important sense, the complaints are always justified, since they show that the complainant feels excluded.[9]

The development from antidiscrimination to inclusiveness has thus been a natural progression, given the basic assumption that people have a right to equality on the relevant dimensions. All attempts to backtrack or return to a supposedly purer colorblind and sex-blind standard have failed. Once antidiscrimination is accepted as a basic authoritative principle, its demands become ever more radical and take on obsessive importance throughout social life. If you are not part of the solution, then simply by living your life from day to day you are cooperating with institutionalized discrimination and making yourself part of the problem. It is therefore not useful in general to distinguish the attempt to suppress discrimination from full-blown inclusiveness, and I will not usually do so.

---

9 According to the influential report on the Lawrence case in London, racism is conduct that is perceived as racist. See the discussion in Green and Grieve, *Institutional Racism and the Police.*

Justifications

We have seen that the attempt to do away with discrimination quite naturally leads to inclusiveness and similar features of contemporary advanced liberalism. But why try to do away with it? The immediate answer is that discrimination is just obviously wrong. Why treat Joe worse than Bob for some irrelevant reason, especially one Joe cannot do anything about?

The question, though, is why people believe that choosing Bob over Joe is treating Joe badly, why sex, religion, ethnicity, and the like should be irrelevant to human connections, and why the issues are so clear-cut that disagreement shows inexcusable ignorance, stupidity, malice, or psychological disorder. A variety of responses to that question have been proposed, mainly implicitly, since the question itself rarely comes up.

Protection Against Injury

A common view among ordinary people is that discrimination is obviously injurious to those discriminated against. If someone cannot get an education or a job, because people will not admit or hire him, this is an injury. If afterwards he has trouble making his way in the world, the injury very likely caused the problem. History seems to confirm the point. Blacks, who have been subject to severe discrimination, have always been poorer than other Americans. Irish Catholics were subject to disabilities in Ireland and they starved. The Jews were often quite poor, when they were forced to live in ghettos or the Pale of Settlement. All those groups are doing better, now that discrimination is illegal.

The argument seems obvious, but it is much weaker than thought. Extreme forms of discrimination like pogroms and extensive civil disabilities are certainly injurious. Where they are found, though, antidiscrimination laws are not likely to be the answer, since such laws will exist only where basic conditions are mostly favorable to minorities. If influential people want nothing to do with minority group members, laws protecting them from discrimination will not be adopted. If there are enough influential people who do not mind dealing with them for the laws to pass and take effect, they will not be in much economic danger in any event. Instead of a thousand possible employers they might have 600, who will hire them because they want them as workers rather than through compulsion. Their wages might be somewhat depressed because they have less choice among employers, but that would make them more attractive as employees so the effect will tend to vanish.[10]

The point is borne out by comparison of the state of minorities before and after the adoption of antidiscrimination measures. The Jews, Chinese, and Irish were discriminated against in America, but prospered. To do so, they did not need equal social acceptance, only civil rights as traditionally conceived: the right to own property, enforce contracts, engage in business, and so on. In contrast, blacks and Hispanics have been the beneficiaries of affirmative action programs for forty years, and in important respects their problems have become worse. The Civil Rights Act of 1964 was enacted after a long period of black progress and during the early stages of a general movement of social transformation that soon led to large-scale rejection of traditional social arrangements of all kinds. This movement would have had a profound effect on racial attitudes and practices, even if its principles had not been made legally compulsory. Even so, black economic and social progress stagnated after the early '70s. With that in mind, what are the grounds for praising the Civil Rights Act as a turning point that led to a radically beneficial social transformation?[11]

Historical Justice

Many aspects of inclusiveness, especially racial preferences in hiring, are commonly justified by reference to historical justice: whites have treated blacks badly, so whites are suspect, and whatever problems blacks have should be attributed to them. The alternative would be to blame the victim, leave the effects of past injuries in place, and carry forward prejudices that have been used to support injustice.

The line of thought is rather sweeping and leaves important

---

10 See Block, *The Case for Discrimination.*

11 See, e.g., Thernstrom and Thernstrom, "Black Progress." Also see 'Specific Groups,' pp. 122 ff. below.

questions unanswered. Which whites? Which blacks? How badly? In what respects? Where is the causality? How do other situations fit in? And what about now?[12] Some whites certainly did treat some blacks badly. Slavery is an evil. Violent enforcement of racial subordination is wrong. On the other hand, there are many things that do not fit the grand drama of white sin and black victimization. Whites have often aided blacks either specifically or through general public service. They have cured disease, raised living standards, increased life expectancy, provided relatively honest and efficient government, and suppressed crime and slavery among black people. There were whites who never had any contact with blacks and others who died to free slaves. To all appearances, blacks who live in majority white countries are better off than those who live in majority black countries, and those who vote with their feet confirm the judgment.[13] Since whites who vote with their feet also prefer to live among whites, it seems clear that blacks benefit from whites more than whites from blacks, and the view that race relations are a matter of whites exploiting blacks makes no sense.

Also, blacks often act badly themselves. There are proportionally far more black criminals than white, and they prey on members of both races, blacks more than whites, since blacks are closer at hand.[14] Some whites held slaves, but it was black Africans who sold them the slaves. Indeed, some American blacks owned slaves as well, and it was a 1654 case in law brought by a black Virginia slaveholder, Anthony Johnson, that established black slavery as perpetual.

Nor is it clear what black history has to do with other groups,

12 For an argument that distinguishes sharply between causes, which may well involve the conduct of whites, and remedies, which must emphasize the conduct of blacks, see Wax, *Race, Wrongs, and Remedies: Group Justice in the 21st Century*.

13 About 165 million people, or 38 percent of the population of sub-Saharan Africa, say they would migrate internationally, mostly to white countries, if the opportunity arose. Esipova and Ray, *700 Million Worldwide Desire to Migrate Permanently*. In contrast, very few blacks migrate from majority white to majority black countries.

14 *The Color of Crime: Race, Crime and Justice in America*.

Mexicans for example. The Mexican War may have been unjust, but there has been a peace treaty in place for 160 years, and it is unclear why the descendants of Indians and Spanish settlers south of the Rio Grande should have special rights with regard to northern lands to which neither they nor their ancestors ever had any real connection. It is still more unclear what connection women or Third World immigrants have with the history of American blacks or other serious historical injustices.

In any event, historical guilt cannot be the real explanation for the peculiar status of inclusiveness in public morality today. If one people injures another, is this a reason for abolishing the separate existence of peoples? Are there no other considerations to take into account? Also, the basis of historical guilt shifts opportunistically, and it is assessed quite differently in different settings. In Europe, guilt is due to Hitler and colonialism, in America to slavery and segregation. In contrast, blacks are not subject to guilt for the bad conduct of blacks, Indians for what their ancestors did to other Indians, environmentalists for the ravages of malaria, nor progressives for atrocities committed by the Jacobins, Bolsheviks, Chinese Communists, or Khmer Rouge.[15] Guilt may motivate some people, but it is a consequence rather than cause of their understanding of group relations. The real basis of antidiscrimination and inclusiveness must lie elsewhere.

Common Humanity

Supposed deep thinkers often put forward the view that inclusiveness manifests broadening recognition of common humanity and therefore represents fundamental moral progress. The view is an odd one. A denial of common humanity is a possible source of different treatment, but not the only one. If Bob avoids unreliable people, he is not denying their humanity. Why should the conclusion be different, if he believes Irishmen are unreliable and avoids them? His conduct might be ill-founded and ill-natured, but it hardly suggests he believes the Irish are not human. The claim is even more bizarre when applied, as it often is, to the rela-

---

15 See Panné et al., *The Black Book of Communism*, for the truly staggering death toll attributable to communist regimes.

tion between the sexes. Who can read pre-1970s literature or talk to older people and conclude that before the rise of contemporary feminism women were not considered fully human?

At bottom, the thought seems to be that believing that there are human distinctions that matter denies common humanity. The thought may come out of a skeptical way of thinking that tells us that, where there are differences, it is futile to look for some common essence like "humanity" to put things back together. Or it may be that self-definition is thought to make us human, and to categorize people is to deny them self-definition. Either way, the problem, if it exists, is universal and unavoidable. Social organization requires distinctions, which exclude, and, if you get rid of one, another takes its place. The Supreme Court is more "inclusive" than it used to be, since it includes blacks, women, and Hispanics, but the result is that it excludes everyone except Jews and Catholics who graduated from Yale or Harvard Law School. More to the point, it would not exist as the Supreme Court, if the justices did not have immense powers in which others do not share. In Supreme Court arguments the justices sit above, while the lawyers have to stand below, use special forms of address, and submit without complaint to constant interruption. Does that show that the whole institution is essentially dehumanizing and should be abolished?

In fact, the view that contemporary inclusiveness means a broader recognition of common humanity demonstrates a lack of self-knowledge possible only to a ruling class that is self-satisfied to the point of blindness. As things are, if Bob prefers to associate with white Evangelicals and Rob prefers to associate with liberal graduates of prestigious universities, Rob's standards exclude many more people than Bob's. In spite of that, he is likely to believe that he has a broader recognition of common humanity and that Bob is rather a bigot.

Avoiding Hurtfulness

For many people the strongest motive for supporting inclusiveness is avoidance of what gives offense. To oppose it is to allow and indeed cause some people to feel excluded. Avoiding offense and assuring people they are wanted are specifically feminine impulses, and the feminization of public discussion no doubt explains part of the strength of the motive.

That cannot be the ultimate explanation, of course, since feelings of sympathy do not exist in isolation. When there is offense, it matters who is offended, and people sympathize where sympathy is considered appropriate. No one would care if an ordinary taxpayer was offended because he was excluded from participation in a faculty meeting at the state university. Also, feminization is an adaptation to other social changes that make feminine characteristics useful to people who run things. Masculine virtues have less of a function, when all basic decisions have already been made through judicial, bureaucratic, and commercial institutions thought to embody neutral rationality. Under such circumstances, feminine concerns such as avoiding hurtfulness and making life pleasant within an order others have created seem more to the point.

Whatever its ultimate source, an emphasis on avoiding hurtfulness is a useful rhetorical ploy. It disables opposition, since to object to inclusiveness is itself hurtful. That is why it is so important in academic settings: it silences intellectual opposition by making truth irrelevant. It also does away with limits on what can reasonably be demanded, since people sensitive to slights will find them everywhere. Colin Powell thought he was a victim of racial profiling at National Airport, when he was not recognized immediately as national security advisor. Henry Louis Gates, Jr. felt threatened by racist violence, when a policeman in Cambridge, Massachusetts, came to his door and asked to speak with him. If the hurt feelings and irrational alarm suffered by these extremely privileged men demonstrate the intolerable racism of white society, then there is no limit to what may have to be done to set things right.

Claims of insult are often enough colorable, of course. Other people do not care about us nearly so much as we do about ourselves, so to mix with others is to suffer slights. And being excluded is painful, in the same way rejection in courtship and any number of other things are painful. On the other hand, the current situation, in which blacks and other members of protected classes spend their lives working with people whom they suspect would rather have nothing to do with them, does not make its beneficiaries happy either.[16] It requires people to deal with each other in the face of an underlying tension that has to be papered over at all costs, so that human relations become artificial and infinitely fraught. The result, unfortunately, is to create a demand for ever more comprehensive measures to overcome residual problems. Like other social programs, inclusiveness entrenches itself by exacerbating the problems it purports to overcome.

In any event, there is always discrimination. Affirmative action discriminates on the reverse of the traditional grounds. A commercial, bureaucratic, and supposedly merit-based society like our own discriminates on grounds of money, position, and formal certification. People compete ferociously for those prizes, so they must find it painful to be excluded from them.[17] It is not possible even in theory to get rid of discrimination and exclusion. If there were no laws against them, people who wanted to work together would find each other. In the long run, this would bring about more happiness than current arrangements.

Promotion of Community

A somewhat related argument for inclusiveness is that it promotes community in a fragmented world. To be part of a community is to be included in it, so that a maximum of inclusion seems likely to promote a maximum of community.

A problem with the argument is that community is less a matter of abolishing divisions than establishing ties that are intertwined with common goals and standards. There are a great many distinctions among the members of a hierarchical church or an army at war. These are nonetheless communities, because the distinctions are functional, and they relate to networks of close personal connections, and to common goals to which the members attribute extreme importance.

---

16 For details, see Cose, *The Rage of a Privileged Class: Why Are Middle-Class Blacks Angry? Why Should America Care?*

17 See Cobb and Sennett, *The Hidden Injuries of Class*, for an account of how meritocracy looks to blue-collar workers.

In fact, inclusiveness destroys community[18] by reducing the importance of personal ties, making us interchangeable with others and making our goals as much a matter of individual choice as possible. There is nothing special to distinguish shoppers at a shopping mall from each other, so there are no divisions among them. They do not constitute a community, however, because there is nothing that brings them together other than a common interest in acquiring consumer goods. Each has come for his own purposes. They have very few positive duties toward one another and they could just as easily be somewhere else, if they found some minor advantage in being so.

What applies to shoppers at a shopping mall also applies to clients of a social welfare bureaucracy and the taxpayers who fund it. There are no strong personal ties or commitments among such people, since each of them is simply pursuing his own goals within a general legal scheme intended to increase his independent ability to do so.[19] Since that is so, how can inclusiveness and the market and bureaucratic institutions it favors promote community? Everyone is included, but, the more automatic and impersonal the inclusion, the less community people feel.

Practical Benefits

It is often claimed that diversity and inclusiveness have positive consequences that make them immensely valuable.[20] They are

18 On the general point, see Putnam, "E Pluribus Unum: Diversity and Community in the Twenty-first Century."

19 Compare Berggren and Trägårdh, "The Nordic Way: Social Trust and Radical Individualism":

> an overarching ambition in the Nordic countries [is] not to socialize the economy but to liberate the individual citizen from all forms of subordination and dependency within the family and in civil society: the poor from charity, the workers from their employers, wives from their husbands, children from parents—and vice versa when the parents become elderly...legislation has made the Nordic countries into the least family-dependent and most individualized societies on the face of the earth.

20 See Wood, *Diversity: The Invention of a Concept*, for a general discussion. For a much less positive view than the one Wood describes, see Jaeger, *Paideia: The Ideals of Greek Culture*, pp. 218–219, 236:

> [Plato] thought that the *worst* thing that could happen was the mingling of all Greek stocks with one another. He held that was just as bad as the mingling of

said to make us strong, vibrant, and creative by encouraging multiple perspectives that come together to give us the best way of dealing with every situation. In fact, they do nothing of the kind. Multiculturalism tries to combine unity and diversity by celebrating differences, while eliminating their relevance to social functioning. The solution is misconceived. Emphasis on differences creates disunity, and attempting to eliminate their effect suppresses the natural ways people connect and function. The result is a chaotic hodge-podge forced into an artificial order by bureaucracy, propaganda, therapy, and money.

Matters are made worse by the hostility to informal local initiatives that is inevitable in a multiculturalist society. If people are allowed to work out matters with each other based on informal habits and common sense, events will be heavily influenced by local prejudices and power differentials. To prevent such a result, thought and action must be brought into a single scheme managed from the top, with local discretion subject to detailed supervision and second guessing. The resulting state of affairs will be neither vibrant nor creative, but crude, clueless, boring, bureaucratic, and arbitrary—the very opposite of what was hoped for.

Inclusiveness homogenizes. Unity in diversity is a complex business that cannot be imposed from above or achieved by formula. The natural tendency is for social authorities to try to achieve common goals, while the members and groupings of society try to maintain their particularity and autonomy. At its best, the resulting mixture of struggle, resistance, cooperation, accommodation, and mutual exchange brings about the complex, imperfect, and changing unity in diversity that gives social life the qualities multiculturalism claims to promote, but in fact destroys. Perfect comprehensive solutions never work perfectly. The great ages of creativity have also been great ages of struggle.

Diversity of the kind now celebrated is uncreative for other reasons as well. It offers an array of possibilities that are already worked out and obviate the need to create something new.

Greeks and barbarians. . . . Without Sparta the Greek tribes would have mingled with one another and with the barbarians in utter confusion, like the population of the Persian Empire. For Plato, that is the real meaning of the freedom won in the Persian war.

Instead of trying to cook their own dishes in new ways, people order in from ethnic restaurants.[21] More basically, human creativity does not begin with a *tabula rasa*. It varies and develops what already exists. To do so, it needs to start with something that is coherent as well as multi-leveled and open-ended. Shakespeare responded to Plutarch and other foreign sources, so that he benefited from diversity in this respect, but his setting and background enabled him to transform what he absorbed into something that was not only universal, but English and his own. Such an achievement would have been impossible, if he had only pidgin, bureaucratese, and politically correct dogma to work with.

In addition, the higher levels of creativity require a transcendent reference point that enables us to see our activities in a larger setting within which there is something worthwhile they can express and aspire to. Without such a setting, creativity turns into willfulness. The necessary reference point depends on coherent religious and cultural traditions of a type liberal inclusiveness intentionally demotes and disrupts.[22] In place of such traditions, it imposes a system that aspires only to prosperity, security, and equality and is more suited to bureaucrats than poets. The result is that artistic creativity loses any possible relevance to the social order and takes refuge in rebellion against whatever remains of traditional order, or in minor arts whose lack of importance allows their practitioners to aspire to the good, beautiful, and true.[23] Genre fiction, gardening, and cooking enjoy a comparative golden age, while public arts such as architecture become crude, ugly, and nihilistic.

---

21 Sailer, "Why Multicultural Societies Are Less Creative."

22 Murray, *Human Accomplishment: The Pursuit of Excellence in the Arts and Sciences, 800 BC to 1950*, argues that creativity requires recognition of transcendental goods such as the good, beautiful, and true, and notes it has tended to decline since the dawn of liberal society around the end of the 18th century.

23 Even the minor arts can at times become political. In horticulture, for example, some commentators see an emphasis on native species as implicitly racist. See, e.g., Coates, *American Perceptions of Immigrant and Invasive Species: Strangers on the Land*; Pollan, "Against Nativism."

The Multiculturalism of Fear

If someone doubts the arguments for inclusiveness already mentioned, the horrendous evils threatened by discrimination and exclusion are thought to decide the issue. The latter practices are said to be irrational, disruptive, and dangerous to the highest degree. Simply by being what they are, they are thought to lead to Auschwitz.

False Fears

Such claims are evidently false. Institutions and societies necessarily discriminate and exclude. Social harmony and efficiency are aided by distinct roles, accepted boundaries, and settled relationships of authority. Such things help maintain stability and the social connections and distinctions that let people live in a way that fits their special qualities and interests and fosters community as well as genuine diversity.

So discrimination of some sort is inevitable. Discrimination on the grounds now forbidden is a human universal, and there is no evident reason why it is more closely connected to political disaster or radical evil than discrimination on other grounds. The Holocaust was an instance of atrocious treatment on account of race. It was also an instance of atrocious treatment on account of an ideological myth regarding the exploitation of man by man. The latter is a better description, since it brings out the similarity to other recent episodes of industrialized mass murder, most of which have been committed in the service of left-wing progressivism. The opponents of the Nazis who were most progressive, humanitarian, and universalist in their stated ideals were, in the name of those ideals, as murderous as the Nazis themselves. Instead of killing Jews, they killed presumed counterrevolutionaries.

Since that is so, why are traditional distinctions uniquely dangerous and movements to eradicate them uniquely hopeful? The Left has discovered the trick of attributing all evil to whatever perennial feature of life they currently want to do away with: religion, the family, private property, the profit motive, ethnic distinctions. In each case, the feature they want to get rid of can be presented as a collection of invidious distinctions that lead to oppression and resentment: we and they, my family and yours, true religion and false, my property and the property of others. The problem is that principles of social order always make distinctions that can be described invidiously and applied tyrannically: my reason and your bigotry, my public spirit and your self-seeking, my good ideas and your bad ones. Do away with the possibility of invidious description, and there would be nothing left of social order.

In reality, the leftist attack on particularities of religion, kinship, ethnicity, and property is an attack on any principle of local autonomous functioning that stands in the way of total bureaucratic control over social life. Attempts to abolish such principles of resistance have repeatedly led to tyranny, degradation, and murder. There is no reason to support these and, indeed, every reason to oppose them. Why give such attempts presumptive moral authority?

Is the Remedy Beneficial?

A basic problem with the argument from fear is that, if conditions make serious oppression likely, laws against discrimination and the like will not be enacted and enforced. The problem in Germany in 1933–1945 was not the absence of laws against hate speech. Such laws existed in Germany while the Nazis were rising to power, but the conditions that gave the Nazis their appeal made them ineffective.[24] Similarly, the Soviet Union proclaimed draconian penalties for antisemitism,[25] but it was Stalin's death and not Soviet law that saved Soviet Jews from destruction.

Life has risks, and we must deal with it as it is. All social institutions differentiate among persons and cases, and so they all discriminate. Sex and ethnic culture are basic to social functioning. Thus, sex and ethnic discrimination is universal. Outbursts of mass murder and the like therefore need to be explained by

---

24 Bookbinder, "Weimar Germany: The Republic of the Reasonable."

25 In a 1931 letter, Stalin asserted that active antisemitism was punishable by death in the Soviet Union. Stalin, "Reply to an Inquiry of the Jewish News Agency in the United States."

reference to something other than "racism," "sexism," and "homophobia." On the whole, it seems more sensible to explain atrocities by reference to fanaticism, that is to say, the determination to extirpate some basic feature of life, rather than the direction the fanaticism happens to take. Fanatical rejection of ethnic diversity led to Auschwitz, of class differences to the Gulag. Why pretend that one is thoroughly evil, while the other is basically good?

The usual objection to arguments against antidiscrimination laws is that they lack reality. They are answered with anecdotes regarding the harsh realities of racism and the like, as well as by claims that civil rights laws brought obvious radical improvements, otherwise unattainable. As we will see below,[26] what passes for reality in this area is largely invented or tendentiously interpreted. It is normal for government to try to mitigate abuses related to basic human tendencies like making distinctions based on sex, culture, ethnicity, and religion. Examples include women's protective legislation and laws against desecration of places of worship. Such efforts are sometimes beneficial, but they cannot be expanded indefinitely and should be viewed no less critically than other government measures. Intentions do not substitute for effects, and government measures should be viewed especially critically when they attempt to change basic ways in which society functions. Boundaries, exclusions, and discriminations are needed to keep communities and their traditions stable and functional. Hence, attempts to abolish them are more likely to disorder than improve human life.

The antidiscrimination regime does not eliminate the power of some over others. It is an attempt to suppress popular attachments and the people who hold them, most of whom have little inclination toward anything genuinely bigoted. As such, it makes power more one-sided by abolishing local and informal arrangements in favor of more formal ones run from the center. Nor does it do anything to abolish hatred and contempt. Liberal opponents of discrimination have plenty of hatred and contempt for "bigots" and "fundamentalists." That being so, the antidiscrimination

26 See 'Specific Groups,' pp. 122 ff. below

regime seems likely, in the usual manner of utopian movements, to increase rather than reduce the risk of abuse and oppression.

The answer to the genuine risk of disaster from imbalance among the constitutive factors of human life is not a utopian scheme from which everything that can go wrong has been eliminated. It is the attempt to maintain the balance and fend off whatever threats seem greatest. Evil is not a distinct thing that can be identified, isolated, and wiped out. It is a disorder, and a structure as complex as human life can be disordered in many ways. The attempt to identify evil with some one principle, so that it can be extirpated, leads to an uncomprehending extremism that itself becomes a principle of evil. That is especially true, when the principle identified as the source of all evil is intrinsic to social life, like private property, like the existence of groups that resist inclusion in an ideal scheme, and like discrimination based on sex and cultural heritage. The intolerant utopianism of civil rights lawyers has a great deal in common with the tendencies that led to the political catastrophes of the last century. To view their demands as an expression of justice and humanity is a fundamental error.

Opponents of antidiscrimination laws need not claim that exclusion is always good or never abusive, only that it is a normal social function that cannot be done away with. Conduct relating to human differences can be destructive, but the same is true of conduct relating to sex, money, power, or anything else. The proper conclusion is not that basic features of human life should be abolished, but that they should be seen as part of an overall system of things, so that their place in the world can be limited, regularized, and put into perspective.

The Need for Social Peace

A final argument for inclusiveness is that it is needed for social peace. In a diverse society, it is said, resentments arise easily and are likely to build up and lead to very serious problems, unless everything possible is done to minimize divisions and inequalities.

This worry cannot be the fundamental reason for inclusiveness. For the public at large, worries about social peace may be a motive, but for those involved in promoting inclusiveness they are a means. Supporters of the movement intentionally increase diversity through mass immigration and inflame group resentments by publicizing real or invented injustices. They can then gain their point by presenting opposition to inclusiveness as a breach of the social contract and a virtual declaration of war.

In fact, the divisiveness of a position cannot be separated from its merits. Inclusiveness is no different from communism in this regard. If strict equality on some dimension of human life makes for a happier and more peaceful society, then opposition is divisive. If distinctions are necessary for social functioning, then it is the attempt to destroy them that divides. The antidiscrimination laws, as many have noted, serve an educative function by leading people to believe that it is right to insist on certain forms of equality. Doing away with these laws would imply recognition that such a state of affairs is neither possible nor desirable. If people came to accept such a view, it could well improve social peace by eliminating the grievance industry, so that race, sex, and similar characteristics could recede to whatever degree of importance they derive from everyday attitudes based on ordinary experience and practicalities.

Problems would remain, just as problems remain when we reject anarchism and accept government coercion or reject communism and accept economic inequality, but it seems likely the result would be less rancorous and oppressive than what we have now. It is normally best to let men choose their associates, live the way they find natural and worthy of attachment and take whatever comes of it. If they are clannish, there are likely to be reasons for it, and attempts to suppress the inclination are likely to be oppressive and ineffectual. An inclusivist society denies the freedom to associate and forces religious and social conservatives, as well as ethnics attached to inherited ways and loyalties, to treat their religion, ethnic culture, and moral traditions as irrelevant to everything that matters. Groups that increase social diversity are allowed to insist on their particularity to some extent, but the concession is subordinate to the goal of disrupting the cultures of other more dominant groups. Once that goal is accomplished, it will be the turn of the Muslims and black churches to see their own cultures forcibly disrupted for the sake of a yet greater degree of liberation from oppressive social distinctions.

Such a situation is obviously oppressive. A non-inclusivist society that allows such groups to maintain their own ways and thrive through a combination of adaptation and niche-finding seems likely to be less so. The ease of communication and fluidity of life today reduce the danger of abuse and oppression, as well as making self-organization less difficult than in the past. Someone excluded from one part of a non-inclusivist society will likely have better luck elsewhere; those excluded everywhere could develop their own institutions. Loyalties would normally be based on a combination of family, religion, locality, ethnicity, occupation, class, and so on, without one assuming unique power and radically dividing the society. Those who want to limit their common life with others could remain on good terms by keeping out of each other's way, while coming together to deal with common issues. The rule of law and general principles of voluntary ordering would still be available to prevent extremes, allowing a great deal of diversity in a variety of levels and dimensions within a common legal order.

Such an approach would do more to promote peace and freedom than the current approach of suppressing small-scale systems in the interests of a universal homogeneous order. Maintaining a reasonable degree of amity would be recognized for what it is, a political task, rather than something amenable to a final solution by force of law. Even when acceptance of distinctions leads to political separation, the separation of Norway from Sweden and Slovakia from the Czech Republic show that it can be a peaceful process that leads to a new form of stability. Disorders resulting from the collapse of British India and the Soviet Union could better be blamed on the inclusion of incompatible groups within a single political order than on particularism as such. Switzerland, which devolves power and multiplies political divisions that correspond to local, ethnic, and religious differences, is a better model for the future than more centralized arrangements.

4

Why Such Strength?

For proponents of inclusiveness, any argument is good enough. Even if accounts of the benefits of inclusiveness and evils of discrimination are false, they are true in a larger sense, because they tell us that diversity is good and traditional order, which involves distinctions of sex, ethnic affiliation, and so on, is evil and pathological.[1] Facts that derogate from that truth are irrelevant distractions, and mentioning them shows bad motives or fundamental ignorance of social reality.

Social Factors

Why such determined support for the antidiscrimination principle, when there seems to be so little to be said for it? Its supporters often appeal to particular evils to which discrimination based on non-liberal distinctions gives rise, but the principle demands a total reconstruction of human relations that goes far beyond any response to such problems. It is a religion, and something more fundamental is needed to explain it.

---

1 In connection with the Tawana Brawley hoax, which related to the claimed abduction and rape of a black teenager by several white men, the anthropologist Stanley Diamond argued in *The Nation* that "it didn't matter whether the crime occurred or not," because it described what "actually happens to too many black women." Diamond, "Reversing Brawley." Actually, of course, the rape of black women by white men is rare and gang rape practically unknown. See references cited in Auster, "The Truth of Interracial Rape in the United States."

Class Interest

Part of the explanation for the power of inclusiveness is class interest. Liberalism is power that hides itself. In order to make good on its claim to achieve equality and combine it with freedom and democracy, it must keep the people from causing problems by exercising their freedom. "Celebrating diversity" helps it do so by insisting that all beliefs and cultures be given equal credit. The result is that none of them can be allowed to affect anything that matters. All significant decisions must be made by someone who can pass himself off as an outside authority applying neutral standards of human rights, economic efficiency, and administrative effectiveness.

It is not surprising that people able to present themselves that way support inclusiveness. It destroys informal standards and distinctions and so makes it much harder for traditional institutions and informal arrangements to function. Expertise, bureaucracy, money, and the state become the only serious principles of order, and the verbal, credentialed, well-placed, and rich end up running everything.

The self-interested nature of elite support for inclusiveness is usually not overt or even conscious. Experts and managers believe in their own way of doing things and view its extension as an obvious good. They see the replacement of traditional arrangements by markets and rational management as a matter of destroying prejudice, opening up opportunities, and using manpower rationally. The same process can, of course, be viewed as the destruction of cultural understandings, relationships, and ways of doing things, and their replacement by formal institutions and procedures that are incomprehensible to those at the bottom and easily controlled by those at the top.

Human Vulnerability

Inclusiveness appeals to the powerless as well as the powerful. Modern industrial society dissolves human connections and so isolates people and puts them at the mercy of large impersonal structures. Under such circumstances, it is natural for people to want security against abuse and misfortune and to look to government, the only structure strong enough to be counted on, to provide it. Equal treatment seems the most reliable standard, since other standards have no solid basis in a society that denies substantive principles of social order.

The connection between political outlook and personal connectedness demonstrates the strength of such considerations. The big political divisions in America are those between the married and unmarried, churchgoers and the secular, and big-city ("Blue State") people and their somewhat more countrified cousins. In each case, those attached to particular individuals, small-scale structures, and transcendent loyalties are conservative, while those dependent on rationalized, cosmopolitan, this-worldly structures are liberal.[2] The effect of such differences is greater among women, who often feel vulnerable and take social setting and personal connections more seriously.[3]

Inclusiveness thus assuages worries brought on by present-day tendencies, but makes the underlying problems worse by increasing the impersonality of institutions, the pervasiveness and inhumanity of bureaucracy, and the isolation of individuals, as well as their total dependence on state and market. The source of its relative stability is that it feeds the problems that create it. It is a black hole into we have fallen and from which we seemingly cannot escape.

Background Understandings

Fear and self-interest are strong influences, but neither is adequate to explain the strength of the trend toward inclusiveness. It is difficult to persuade people that objections to it are even possible, and something that seems so irrefutably correct to so many intelligent people must be rooted in fundamental ways of viewing the world.

---

2 See Franc, "Democrats Wake up to Being the Party of the Rich."

3 A poll during the 2012 presidential campaign, for example, gave Barack Obama a 2-1 lead over Mitt Romney among single women, while the two were almost even among voters generally, and Romney led 51 to 38 percent among married people. Jensen, "Obama Tops Romney in Poll With 2-1 Backing From Single Women."

Technology

To a large extent, the appeal of inclusiveness results from a technological outlook that makes discrimination seem irrational and its legal eradication practical and reasonable for the following reasons:

• Mass markets, mass education, the welfare state, and other large impersonal institutions eliminate local arrangements and the relevance of local knowledge. The social order comes to seem a straightforward overall structure to be organized and reorganized by reference to universal standards.

• Television and the Internet abolish privacy, particularity, and settled connections. They fragment experience, put every fragment on a par, make every point on earth equally present to every other, and let people reassemble the fragments however they want.

• Easy travel, mass tourism, global markets, and the instability of employment dissolve stable local relationships in favor of individual choice within a universal abstract order that treats everything as interchangeable with everything else.

• Electronic entertainment, fast food, and day care replace family life. Pop culture and advertising inculcate self-indulgence and consumerism as all-sufficient goals in life.

Such conditions, which make every social status and connection seem arbitrary and evanescent, are the background of public discussion today. The result is that old norms become incomprehensible. Traditional sexual standards provide an example. Standards that once supported stable local patterns through which people carried on their lives are now considered an irrational violation of universal abstract structures designed to satisfy arbitrary individual choice. The obviously good has become obviously bad. The result is the new definition of "tolerance." A word that once meant putting up with transgression to some extent now means supporting it wholeheartedly. Inherited norms have become illegitimate, so that every transgression of them is considered a victory for rationality and justice.

60

Scientism

Basic principles of social organization correspond to fundamental understandings regarding the world. As we will see in what follows, the basic principle that leads to inclusiveness is a view of reason that critics refer to as scientism or scientific fundamentalism. This view has been with us since the scientific revolution of the seventeenth century and has been transforming social understandings and relationships ever since. The process through which it has been doing so, sometimes called modernization or rationalization, remains ongoing. The abolition of traditional and natural patterns of human life in the name of diversity and inclusiveness is a current manifestation of that process.

REASON

Reason is the orderly process through which we reach well-founded conclusions regarding the good, beautiful, and true. This process is neither simple nor easy, and we always fall short of the ideal in carrying it forward. That is why we habitually rely on easier and more accessible expedients for the practical understandings by which we live: habit, experience, tradition, intuition, rule of thumb, and so on.

These things do not give us comprehensive or perfectly lucid knowledge, but they are systematically related to the truth of things, and we could not think at all without their assistance. Nonetheless, they are incomplete, and problems arise when we treat them as equivalent to reason itself. Such treatment is most often a matter of thoughtless habit, but it can also take the form of positive denial that there is anything higher than the concrete principles we habitually live by. In either case, the result is that our way of understanding loses awareness of its incompleteness and becomes crude and degraded.

Mindless dogmatism, insistence that whatever we habitually believe is unquestionable truth, is a familiar example of such a situation. There are more subtle examples, however, and the scientistic understanding is such a case. Modern natural science provides exact and very useful knowledge. Its insistence on clarity, simplicity, and testability gives it great power. This insistence also renders it incapable of dealing with certain issues, some of which are extremely important.

In particular, it is unable to deal effectively with subjectivity, qualitative matters, and patterns of life that involve complex and subtle matters that resist clear formulation, like those related to sex and culture. Scientism therefore insists that such things be ignored. It is too hard to find out what we naturally want to know, it seems to say, so let us treat something that is easier to study, understand, and make use of as equivalent to reality itself. In short, let us hold that what is not scientific does not exist. And as a matter of social policy, let us get rid of messy distinctions that do not fit the kind of system we can understand and control.

The result is radical simplification of the intellectual and social world that has several aspects: extreme secularization, suppression of traditional arrangements, hypertrophy of rationalized social structures such as world markets and the administrative state, and, most recently, inclusiveness—the insistent abolition of distinctions that are at odds with a fully rationalized social order.

HISTORY

Scientism, or scientific fundamentalism, has deep roots. Its components, such as the insistence on simple, universal, and mechanistic explanations, have been with us since antiquity. These tendencies have led on occasion to views very much like modern scientific materialism.[4] Until modern times, however, such views never enjoyed wide currency. Today they have come together in an outlook that sets the standard for public discussion and holds that modern natural science is the only knowledge worthy of the name. This view is not held explicitly by many people, since few people engage in logical analysis of fundamental issues. The question though is one of public validity rather than private belief. Whatever is thought to be scientific is authoritative and

---

4 Democritus (ca. 460–370 BC) claimed, for example, that "in reality there are only atoms and the void."

trumps everything else. Contrariwise, whatever is not considered such hardly counts for anything at all in public discussion.[5]

It is difficult to trace the exact process by which something as all-embracing as a revised understanding of reason achieves dominance. However, the thought of Francis Bacon (1561–1626) and René Descartes (1596–1650) evidently marked a decisive stage in the rise of the current outlook. Both men aimed at a general intellectual reform that would make knowledge more certain and useful. Bacon, a practically-minded statesman, wanted to reconstruct knowledge on experimental principles for "the relief of man's estate," that is, to make life easier, safer, and more pleasant. He thought that "knowledge is power," and, with that in mind, wanted it to reject tradition, base itself on observation of the natural world, and become a tool. In effect, he wanted it to become modern technology. Descartes, a scientist and mathematician, wanted knowledge that would stand up against any possible objection. He could not doubt the reality of his own subjective experience. As he said so famously, "I think, therefore I am." Thus, he tried to base knowledge on that experience, together with the most rigorous reasoning possible.

Put the two views together and you get a narrow, focused, and, it turns out, extremely effective view of knowledge. On that view, we should be as skeptical as possible and base knowledge and our whole way of thinking and acting as much as possible on our own immediate experience and on mathematics and logic. And we should treat the purpose of knowledge as severely practical. This is to say that it has to do with getting what we want.

Such a view excludes from rationality everything that goes beyond human experience and purpose. The transcendent, it seems to say, is beyond us. We do not know what it is, and there is nothing we can do about it, so why take it into account? Some of the consequences of such a view and the length of the process that has led to the present situation can be seen in the history of

---

5 The Milgram Experiment, in which most ordinary people proved willing to inflict severe torture when instructed to do so by someone identified with the authority of science, demonstrates the status of science in today's world. See Milgram, *Obedience to Authority.*

the word "speculation." The word comes from the Latin *specere*, to "look at" or "view." When it appeared in English around 1374, it meant "contemplation" or "consideration." By 1575, at the dawn of the moderri age, it had taken on the disparaging sense of "mere conjecture." And by the eve of the great modern revolutions, in 1774, it had come to mean "buying and selling in search of profit from rise and fall of market value."[6]

So, in four hundred years, "speculation," attending to things on some basis other than knowledge as power, went from man's noblest faculty, contemplation or speculative reason, to making things up, and from there to trying to get money without knowing what you are up to.

CHARACTERISTICS

Modern natural science has great strengths. It has built-in checks that tend to catch errors. It can be extremely successful when pursued with discipline, attentiveness and ingenuity and so calls forth high-quality intellectual effort. It has solved a great many problems and continues to support fruitful inquiry on a very wide range of topics. However, it narrowly restricts what counts as evidence and proof, and its rigorous attitude toward such issues causes it to take an extremely critical attitude toward tradition, common sense, revelation, and other nonscientific forms of guidance.

Many supporters of modern natural science attempt to universalize this critical attitude. To appeal to any principle outside science, they believe, would compromise an extremely successful strategy of investigation for the sake of some particular concern that may yet be dealt with, to the extent it is legitimate, within science itself. And this, they believe, would be an attack on the process through which we attain knowledge and thus on knowledge itself. To look for reliable public truth from a non-scientific source is, we are told, antiscientific and therefore antirational.[7]

---

6 "Online Etymology Dictionary: Definition of 'Speculation.'"

7 Some such concern seems to be behind extreme and indeed self-destructive claims such as those found in Rosenberg, "The Disenchanted Naturalist's Guide to Reality," which tells us that adequate respect for science requires us to recognize that there is no such thing as belief or the meaning of a sentence.

The result has been a view that limits knowledge and rational guidance to a very few sources, those upon which modern natural science relies most explicitly. These sources are:

• Observations that can be verified by any properly trained observer.

• The assumption of the uniformity of nature, meaning that what happened in the past will happen in the future.

• Formal logic, mathematics, and measurement, which enable us to organize and connect our observations and make them exact, impersonal, and usable. If an observation cannot be made numerical, it is not taken seriously.

• When necessary, additional assumptions that comply with Occam's Razor, that is to say, are as few and simple as possible and can be tested by experiment. Such assumptions are the basis of model building.

Occam's Razor is important. When someone says "you are just trying to force your values on other people," it is an appeal to this principle. You are, it is implied, bringing in some assertion that is neither proved nor needed and so you are being willful and oppressive. In itself, Occam's Razor is a perfectly sensible injunction to keep things simple. Nonetheless, its overly aggressive use can distort inquiry by making it govern reality rather than regulate inference. Rather than tell us to choose the simpler explanation where two explanations work equally well, it is used to rule out explanations that refer to things modern natural science has trouble dealing with. It thus becomes equivalent to the dogmatic claim that modern natural science is sufficient for all our needs, a claim that is, of course, radically unscientific.

CONSEQUENCES

The consequences of trying to understand the world only scientifically pervade present-day life in several ways:

• If what we can know is what can be observed and measured, then that is what we can treat as real. Everything else is feeling, taste, opinion, prejudice, or fantasy.

• The experimental method tells us how events depend on other events that we can control, and so it has to do with the control of nature. Thus, if knowledge essentially has to do with the experimental method, it blends seamlessly into technology.

• Further, science dislikes formal and final cause, that is to say, the essential features of a thing in their mutual relations and the states of affairs they characteristically bring about. Such principles bring in too many imponderables. Who is to say when something is too little horselike to be a horse? And who is to say whether it is the true nature of a horse to crop grass, win races, have offspring, die gloriously in battle, live long and prosper, provide glue and horse meat, or occupy whatever volume of space it actually occupies? Scientism therefore aspires to do without such principles. It prefers to appeal to material and efficient cause, to the thing's physical constituents and the events that directly brought it into being. This aspiration is perpetually frustrated, since without formal and final cause it is impossible to discuss functional systems such as living organisms, but people still try to minimize their use or explain them away.

• Insistence on measurement and control and the rejection of formal and final cause make science unable to deal with evaluative concepts like "good" and "beautiful" on anything like their own terms. To take them seriously, they must be made observable and measurable, and, to do that, they must be identified with observed preferences. But if "good" means "preferred," it is simply a matter of what we want, and its attainment becomes indistinguishable from the triumph of the will.

The result of such tendencies is a comprehensive technological outlook that determines our understanding of the world. An industrial process has no memories or loyalties, and a computer interacts with equal facility with any other computer anywhere for any purpose. The corresponding outlook places us in a sort of eternal now without place, context, or purpose, in which everything is a neutral resource for the achievement of the current

projects of whoever is in control. Stable relationships and purposes dissolve into a haze of technical possibilities.

In such a setting, there are no essential functions or qualities,
no nature of things to underwrite identities, so we create the latter for our own purposes. Self-definition becomes the thing that
makes us more than objects defined by our use in the projects of
others and thus becomes the essence of our dignity. Since getting
what we want is the purpose of thought, to classify someone and
make him part of a general scheme is to treat him as a thing to be
used. In this way, membership in a larger whole comes to seem
an external imposition. Hence arises the belief that traditional
culture, which is always based on particular connections, identities, and meanings, is intrinsically oppressive; that "essentialism,"
the belief that things have a particular nature and significance, is
ignorance and bigotry; and that "discrimination", treating one
connection as more fitting than another for any non-technologi-
cal reason, is irrational and wrong. Different treatment on
account of inborn or inherited qualities and connections
becomes particularly offensive, since the individual does not
choose them. That is why there is such extreme resistance to recognizing innate differences among human beings. Such recognition denies our self-createdness, our I AM THAT I AM, and subjects
us to the schemes of others.[8]

Hence the intrinsic destructiveness of modern culture. Self-
definition is now our essence, but it can have no positive content,
when all definitions have become utterly unstable, and so it can
only be negative. Self-definition therefore takes the form of opposition either to other people or to any remaining limitations on
its own absolute freedom. The choices available for modern
man, apart from confusion and dissipation, are thus reduced to

8 That is why in the EU there is a human right to get your birth registra-
tion changed from "male" to "female" if you have undergone surgery and hor-
mone treatments to make you appear female. The UN Yogyakarta Principles,
unanimously adopted by a very high-level group of human rights experts and
intended to guide the interpretation of international law, take a broader
approach, and make "self-defined gender identity" by itself sufficient for
change of all identity documents.

fascism on the one hand and open-ended cultural rebellion and subversion on the other.

Morality and Politics

An attempt to apply the principles of the modern natural sciences to morality and politics might seem surprising. Those principles are designed to deal with objects in space. Since we often concern ourselves with other things, like the good, beautiful, and true, it seems that the principles of modern natural science should have only limited applicability in human affairs. Nonetheless, we are indeed objects in space, and it follows that we can apply the methods of the modern natural sciences to ourselves. Since we can do so, the scientistic version of Occam's Razor insists that we must do so—exclusively. We must try to rely, not just in the realm of physiology and physical anthropology, but even in politics, morality, and social relations generally, on something as close to scientific reasoning as possible. It is considered irrational to do otherwise.

THE LOGIC OF INCLUSIVENESS

When scientism is applied to morality and politics, it gives us a highest good and highest standard of justice. From these two principles, it is possible to generate a complete political and moral system, one that is extremely simple and rigorous and excludes all distinctions other than those it relies on.[9] It is this system, which is now treated as intellectually and morally compulsory, that gives rise to inclusiveness.

The highest good scientism gives us is satisfaction of desire, also called freedom. Preference and aversion are observable, and they are available as guides. Since this is so, Occam's Razor tells us, why not stick with them and concentrate on setting up a system that gives us what we want and gets rid of what we do not want? Why bring in other standards based on things that are harder to observe and verify, like God, essential qualities, natural

---

9 Hobbes' *Leviathan*, which derives a proto-liberal political theory from atomic materialism, is a pioneering attempt to create such a system.

functions, or the good, beautiful, and true? That, it is thought, would be unscientific and therefore irrational.

The standard of justice that corresponds to the resulting system is equality. What is good is simply what is desired, Occam's Razor has told us, and, since all desires are equally desires, all goods are equally goods. It follows that the desires of all men deserve to be treated equally. To say one man's desires are less valuable than another's is simply to value him less. This is arbitrary, discriminatory, and oppressive. It is the sort of thing that leads to Auschwitz and cannot be allowed.

In effect, scientism tells us that there are no transcendent goods, just desires, that there are no essences of things that we should respect, and that the world is what we make of it. From this it follows that the rational approach to politics, social life, and morality is to treat the world as a resource and turn the social order into a kind of machine for giving people in equal measure whatever they happen to want, as long as what they want fits the smooth working of the machine.

That is the present-day liberal understanding. The correctness of liberalism is thus demonstrable, given the present view of reason. Indications that science is at odds with many egalitarian claims[10] do not matter. Scientism is not science. It functions as a comprehensive approach to reality, so as to satisfy needs that actual science, which has no practical responsibilities and only gives answers when it has them, can ignore. The needs to which scientism relates are humanly more important, so that, where there is a conflict, it is science that has to give way.

The specific features of the liberal order follow from its basic logic. A system based simply on reason is uniquely legitimate. This unique legitimacy gives liberalism an insuperable advantage in political and moral discussion. If you reject it, there is something wrong with you. You are irrational, nihilistic, or Nazi, and probably all three. Since you reject reason, you are not properly

---

10 For collections of evidence, see Cochran and Harpending, *The 10,000 Year Explosion: How Civilization Accelerated Human Evolution*; Rushton, *Race, Evolution, and Behavior: A Life History Perspective*; Jensen, *The g Factor: The Science of Mental Ability*.

part of political discussion and should be excluded or you will corrupt it.[11]

Also, reason is universal. Since liberalism follows from reason, or so it claims, it must be universally applicable. All institutions everywhere must have a clear orientation toward maximizing equality and preference satisfaction, and they must lend themselves to supervision and intervention to correct deviations and irrationalities. It follows that institutions and standards that detract from the unity, clarity, universality, and efficiency of the liberal system must be abolished.

The institutions that measure up to those standards are bureaucracies run on liberal principles and markets that are appropriately monitored and regulated, especially when the bureaucracies and markets are global. In contrast, traditional and local institutions—family, nation, religion, and non-liberal conceptions of personal dignity and integrity—are, from the liberal standpoint:

- Opaque and resistant to outside control. They resist change.

- Not based on expert scientific knowledge. They are ignorant and prejudiced.

- Not oriented toward maximum equal satisfaction of individual preference. They are oppressive.

- Dependent on distinctions and authorities that are not required by liberal market and bureaucratic institutions. The family, for example, depends on distinctions of age, sex, and blood. It follows that such institutions are bigoted and hateful.

Accordingly, liberalism tells us, such institutions must be suppressed, since they make a just, rational, and efficient social order impossible.

Such institutions are also extremely dangerous in the eyes of today's liberals. Rational action is a matter of trying to attain some preference with means chosen in accordance with technical criteria. Race, sex, family, heritage, and the like are neither technical criteria nor simple matters of preference, so that they are not rational guides to action. It follows that they are mindless

---

11 See 'Suppression of Discussion,' pp. 84ff. below.

obsessions with no natural limit to what they might demand. Their natural outcome is something very much like Nazism. For the sake of peace, rationality, and justice, they must either be extirpated or brought into the system of liberal rationality by reducing them to private choices with no consequences for social relations that matter.

Hence inclusiveness, multiculturalism, the celebration of diversity, and so on. Nation and culture must become ethnic cuisine and folk dancing, religion a private discipline, personal therapy, or a poeticized version of advanced liberalism. No culture or religion can matter more than any other, so none can matter at all. The family can get lip service. It is said to be enormously important, when it is useful rhetorically, as in the case of "gay families." In fact, though, it can no longer be treated as a social institution, but as a sentimental arrangement with no special content or purpose and therefore no public function.

An example illustrates the consequences of the liberal view. Suppose an official who accepts scientism and its application to social relations is presented with a claim by a gay rights group that they have a right to live in a society free of homophobic attitudes, and a claim by Christians that they have the right to educate their children in the principles they think right, which include the view that homosexual inclinations are intrinsically disordered. The two claims conflict. Who wins?

Obviously, the gay rights group.[12] The purpose of public authority is to establish justice, which includes defending people from oppressive social structures. Christian morality is at odds with the equal standing of all desires that accept the liberal public order. It is therefore irrational and oppressive and should not be allowed to affect social relations. Further, the point of parental involvement in the upbringing of children is its contribution to

---

12 A straw in the wind is provided by suggestions that the new Alberta Education Act would forbid homeschooling parents from teaching the immorality of homosexual behavior. Craine, *Alberta Backtracks: Parents Can Teach Beliefs on Homosexuality, but Homeschoolers Still Concerned.* Also see Craine, "Ontario Education Minister: Catholic Schools Can't Teach Abortion Is Wrong—That's 'misogyny.'"

their ultimate ability to choose and pursue their own legitimate goals, with the liberal public order the standard of legitimacy. The Christian parents reject this principle, which is all that justifies their authority. So why, from the liberal viewpoint now dominant, should they be allowed to determine their children's education?[13] Why should they even be allowed custody of their children?[14]

THE IMMOVABILITY OF INCLUSIVENESS

Liberals say they believe in reason. On their understanding of reason, their views are correct beyond all possibility of discussion. What part of maximum equal satisfaction of legitimate preferences could any intelligent and well-meaning person have a problem with? And what justification could there be for denying equal citizenship to those who accept the principle of equal citizenship? Opposition to the one rational and just system is not only wrong, but inexcusable. If you oppose it, it can only be for one of the following ignoble reasons:

- You are ignorant, confused, and irrational, since your opposition is opposition to reason.

- You are trying to suppress and exclude other people to get more for yourself, to make yourself look better by comparison, or because you just like abusing people.

- So you are greedy, resentful, oppressive, hateful, or all four.

Such views are fundamental to the present legal and public

---

13 In some European countries, parents are routinely fined, jailed, or deprived of custody for homeschooling. "Swedish Politician Calls for Even Harsher Penalties for Homeschooling." The United States government, and the 6th U.S. Circuit Court of Appeals, do not consider such conduct to constitute a violation of human rights. Leigh Jones, "WORLD | Appeals Court Denies Homeschooling Family's Asylum Claim."

14 In England, a couple who foster-parented three migrant children recently lost them, because the couple were members of the U.K. Independence Party, which favors a restrictive immigration policy. Whittle, "Muzzled Britain." And it was proposed to deprive a married couple of their child at birth because of the mother's past membership in the English Defense League, a right wing protest organization. Jeory, "Why Try to Take Baby From EDL Mother but Not From 'Terrorists'?"

moral order. They are taught in the schools, guide all respectable leadership, and define legitimate statecraft. That is why in much of the West you can now be fined or put in jail for saying there are problems with homosexuality or Islam.

All of us are affected by such views, at least to a degree. It is very hard to avoid falling into the basic assumptions on which the people around us, especially the people who run things, carry on discussions. The most basic of those assumptions is their understanding of reason, which now implies liberal inclusiveness. This is why even people who officially do not accept it, for example, would-be religious traditionalists, slide into accepting it in practice.[15] Public discussion must be based on principles acceptable to all parties, but the only principles liberals will accept for purposes of debating their opponents are stripped-down scientistic principles that, when taken as the basis of discussion, automatically give back an endorsement of liberalism. It follows that liberalism and inclusiveness always win.

To make matters worse, a state that denies the relevance of transcendent standards and natural law to social life denies that there is anything that stands above the political order or that the nature of things limits legitimate political choices. The theoretical intolerance of inclusiveness as an expression of the modern understanding of reason is therefore exacerbated by the unlimited character of the modern state. Those with doubts about the correctness of inclusiveness as theory and public policy should be very worried about what it may lead to.

Ultimate Motivations

As an everyday matter, both liberals and conservatives tend to explain tendencies like inclusiveness by reference to particular

---

15 Consider, for example, the instant termination of John Derbyshire's relation to the supposedly conservative *National Review* for proposing to tell his children things about dealing with black people that correspond to what many black people say they tell their children about whites. See Derbyshire, "The Talk: Nonblack Version." The conservative and historically Catholic *National Review* had tolerated Derbyshire's atheist and pro-abortion views, but his violation of inclusivist sensitivities was too much to bear.

psychological dispositions: liberals are weak-minded or fair-minded, they hate straight white men or injustice, they like to interfere or they believe in reform. People have motives for their actions, and almost any such explanation is likely to explain some particular cases. However, human nature is stable, while political regimes change, and goals and dispositions arise, develop, and are judged reasonable or not in accordance with the particularities of its setting. For that reason, it seems more useful to explain a tendency like inclusiveness by reference to its social and conceptual setting than the state of mind of its supporters, and I have in general tried to do so.

Still, ultimate questions regarding the purposes of human action remain. If it is true that the ultimate explanation of political modernity in general, and liberal inclusiveness in particular, is that men's thoughts have turned from the speculative and transcendent to the practical and this-worldly, why did this happen? Was it because the experiment of doing such was so very successful on its own terms? Or was it because men rejected God? Or maybe a little of each?

Such questions are unavoidable, if difficult to answer definitively. We are all heirs to political modernity, a tradition that is evidently now in crisis, and our response to this crisis will necessarily reflect our understanding of the human factors that lay behind the tradition and made it what it has been. Very likely each will interpret the matter in accordance with his own ultimate commitments and understandings. Those who view God as the *ens realissimum* will view modernity as radically flawed from the beginning. Those who view life as a matter of solving practical problems will be more sympathetic to it and look for ways to salvage as much as possible from the wreckage.

5

Effects of Inclusiveness

Diversity and inclusiveness disrupt particular connections and local networks. The promised goal is the recreation of human relations on a more rational basis that better fosters freedom and diverse identities. The effect, however, is the contrary. Inclusiveness destroys the normal ways people connect to each other, so that they become a mass of essentially unconnected individuals with interests that cannot be expected to harmonize. The results include conflict, disorder, regimentation, mindlessness, and the breakdown of the arrangements and understandings that enable people to know who they are and run their own lives.

Compulsion

Inclusiveness tries to eliminate the social effects of important human differences. When pursued seriously, this effort very quickly becomes tyrannical. "Society" is a network of myriad agents. Inclusiveness, like other aspects of the liberal conception of social justice, attempts to hold the outcome of what all those agents do to an overall standard, as if they were the acts of a single person. Any serious attempt to do so necessarily means a comprehensive scheme of control that is fine-grained enough to govern everyday human interactions and exempt from popular influences and traditional limitations that would otherwise protect and empower prejudice.

The need for compulsion is aggravated by the importance of sex, religion, ethnicity, and similar characteristics in human life. These characteristics determine personal identity, because people find that they matter for how they live. Further, enough important human differences are related to them for free dealings to lead to disproportionate outcomes even in the absence of discrimination. For example, neutral enforcement of laws against violent crime will put many more young black men than elderly Jewish women in prison. Where such disproportions arise, the expectations they engender, if allowed to develop freely, will soon lead to conscious discrimination of a kind now considered outrageous.

The tendency to take such characteristics into account is therefore permanent and pervasive. It is even innate, since babies discriminate on the basis of sex and race.[1] Discrimination thus enduringly reasserts itself, if there is no external force continually at work to suppress it. As time passes and the diversity regime develops, the system of force becomes ever more comprehensive. Any inequality corresponds to a benefit in which some do not share, so that the settings and circumstances thought to demand intervention only multiply. A movement that began with calls for anti-lynching legislation has ended in concerns about micro-inequities and inappropriately directed laughter.[2]

Unreality

Human connections are complicated. Employment decisions, for example, involve judgments of how people will act and affect others in complex and demanding situations. Such judgments involve questions of trust, compatibility, and mutual comprehension. It is impossible to separate such considerations from a sense of people's background and who they are. Antidiscrimination law insists on that separation with respect to basic dimensions of personal identity. Whether you are a man or woman, black or white, Navajo or a Chinese immigrant cannot have a material effect on how you are expected to act or how anyone should deal with you in any setting that matters. If it did and people took it into account, that would be discrimination.

---

1 Bronson and Merryman, "See Baby Discriminate"; Clark, "Three-year-olds Being Labelled Bigots by Teachers as 250,000 Children Accused of Racism."

2 See Weisbuch, Pauker, and Ambady, "The Subtle Transmission of Race Bias via Televised Nonverbal Behavior."

Such a denial of reality, turned into dogma and forced on social relations by all means necessary, makes it impossible for people to deal with each other directly, intelligently, and unaffectedly. Occasionally reality does seep in to some extent. People are expected to be "culturally sensitive," which means they are expected to know stereotypes and act on them in some respects. Institutions are expected to make special accommodations for physical and cultural particularities of members of groups qualifying for "affirmative action." However, no one is allowed to take such things into account in any straightforward way. In particular, no one is allowed to take into account the possibility that natural or cultural differences might make some people less suitable than others in some settings. Diversity, meaning proportional or higher representation of minorities and women, must always be treated as advantageous. Any contrary view, it is thought, would vilify those thought to be excluded and treat them as less than human.

Differences in outcome are therefore seen as intolerable. If more black students get low grades or fewer women pursue the hard sciences, it is considered a gross violation of how things should be. In many settings, the resulting insistence on "closing the gap" has come to outrank all other goals.[3] In education, such an insistence has led to grade inflation, collapse of discipline, and misplaced efforts in general. The logic is obvious. If no one gets disciplined or if discipline is based on "zero tolerance," bias vanishes. If everyone gets an A, disparities disappear, and the schools are a great success in dealing with their most important task. If college is the key to success, then all students have to follow a college preparatory curriculum. And if some students learn nothing from it, this is where additional resources are assumed to be most useful.

---

3 The No Child Left Behind Act reoriented the whole of American public education for the sake of closing educational gaps. A quick Google search for "education" and "closing the gap" will give a more general impression of the importance of this issue in public policy discussions.

Uniformity

Every system needs standards, restrictions, and principles of cohesion, and doing away with some makes others more prominent. Suppressing natural and traditional distinctions means reliance on artificial ones. Enforced diversity, it turns out, is enforced uniformity on a different dimension.

Inclusiveness imposes uniformity of attitude and belief. It puts a growing range of tendencies—white ethnic solidarity is one example, disapproval of homosexuality is fast becoming another—beyond the pale even in private. It also insists on trivializing the distinctions that have traditionally been thought to make people what they are. We are allowed to be different and to respond to differences in others only if the differences do not matter. All social institutions must make equal use of every possible kind of person, so persons and settings must be made interchangeable. If Swedish and Italian workplaces are different, this has to change, because otherwise they will be more suited to some people than others. People must be transformed as well. Every soccer mom, drag queen, black Muslim, Christian fundamentalist, and Hmong immigrant has to be retooled to fit in equally well everywhere.

This being the goal, inclusiveness reduces ethnic culture to ethnic-themed fast food, religion to self-indulgent reverie or a poeticized version of liberalism, and marriage to a sentimental recognition of almost any human connection with sexual overtones. The end result is a single liberal way of life based on career, consumption, and diversion variously accessorized in ways not allowed to matter. In theory we are free to pursue whatever ideal of life we prefer. The freedom is insubstantial, however, since the pursuit must be private, whereas ideals of life involve other people. A private ideal of marriage, religion, or public service makes no sense.

The way of life that results is radically at odds with how human goods come about, because it tries to achieve all goods equally for all people. This is impossible, because no person or society can realize all possibilities. We are finite creatures who become good, happy, productive, creative, and so on by becoming something in particular. We realize ourselves not simply as human beings, but as human beings of a particular kind in a particular setting. An account of human achievement is not simply a list of individual cooks, craftsmen, painters, musicians, and thinkers. It is also an account of Cantonese cuisine, Islamic architecture, Italian opera, Chola sculpture, and German philosophy. What applies to the heights of culture applies to its plains and valleys as well. Everyday virtues like courtesy and generosity take form and become concrete in the standards of particular communities. These standards may be equally demanding in Kew, Kiev, and Kyoto, but they are not exactly the same. To try to make them the same is to destroy them and the goods they once helped promote.

Local Paralysis

Inclusiveness suppresses self-organization and voluntary initiatives of all kinds. If local networks and activities are allowed to have an effect, the benefits of social life will depend on particular connections in which some do not participate. If I do something for brother Tom, cousin Dick and neighbor Harry will be left out. This cannot be allowed, so I must be trained not to act that way.

Common Sense

The problems go quite deep. If ordinary people are to act effectively on their own, informal good sense must be accepted as a generally sound basis for action. Inclusiveness cannot allow this, because "the good sense of the people" is shot through with distinctions and inferences that arise in the informal give and take of daily life, and thus with popular prejudices. Inclusiveness means that people must act on principles prescribed by their betters rather than their own understandings. This is one reason special training is required for everything today. It is also the reason for the constant changes in language. Everything has to be renamed, so that "sex" becomes "gender" and the "Koran" the "Qu'ran." The point is not to improve clarity or accuracy, or even to avoid offense, but to force listeners to recognize the speaker as expert and themselves as ignorant laymen with no right to an opinion of their own.

The suppression of independent thought and action by ordinary people necessarily leads to degradation of functional communities, families, and individuals. Our rulers view this as a good thing, implicitly if not consciously. It suppresses arrangements that compete with the liberal state, frees individuals from traditional connections that are viewed as irrational and discriminatory, and clears the way for a rational and just ordering of society devised by those who know better.

Family Life

Family life provides an example of the effect of inclusiveness on informal local structures. Men and women differ, and connections between them that build on those differences are basic to all societies. To forbid sex discrimination is to forbid responding to the differences coherently and unaffectedly. It also makes it impossible to provide social definition and support for settled relationships between the sexes. Such relationships become a private matter no different from any informal connection among individuals. The result is to deprive marriage and the family of specific structure and function. They become names for a variety of arrangements, none of which has any authority, because none can be treated as better than any other.

The consequence is destruction of definite family responsibilities, fostering distrust between the sexes, fragmented and dysfunctional families, impoverished adults, and badly raised, often abused, children. The official response to such problems, apart from further attacks on sexual and other distinctions, is extension of bureaucratic social welfare systems that displace local arrangements and networks. This response further undercuts family and community life by depriving them of their functions and so makes matters worse in the long run.[4]

There are general social tendencies that weaken family life today, such as the industrialization of economic life and social relations generally, but the process is not simply automatic. Natural tendencies that are as basic as those relating to sex keep returning. Thus, what counts as progress requires continual sup-

---

4 The writings of family scholar Allan C. Carlson are helpful on this point.

pression of attitudes and habits that support and order family life. Useful and admirable traits like the tendency of men to work harder and of women to emphasize domestic concerns, once they are married with children, become vices to be eradicated.[5] They support a sexual division of responsibility that is radically at odds with inclusiveness and what now counts as social justice.

Organizational Life

In addition to families, a free society requires a variety of institutions that are independent of government and capable of calling it to account. The variety is not only a check on government, but a source of social strength. What hurts some organizations helps others, and society as a whole is held harmless. Inclusiveness destroys this variety. The demand that every institution become equally welcoming to every group and recruit preferentially from those that are underrepresented severely compromises institutional identity and independence. The imposition of government supervision of hiring and promotion and the increasing uniformity of permitted opinions in academic,[6] media[7] and other settings illustrate the damage inclusiveness inflicts on self-governing institutions and, through them, on society at large.

Inclusiveness damages institutional effectiveness as well as independence. One way it does so is by suppressing standards of competence and concern for achievement. Another is by forbidding treatment of any particular culture as authoritative, so that

---

5 Indeed, Larry Summers' point seems to have been that lesser feminine commitment to scientific work due to family responsibilities did not mean lesser female success should be tolerated. It meant that the success gap should be dealt with and closed with that cause in mind. Also see Desai, Chugh, and Brief, "Marriage Structure and Resistance to the Gender Revolution in the Workplace," which sounds the alarm about "a heretofore neglected pocket of resistance to the gender revolution in the workplace: married male employees who have stay-at-home wives."

6 See Jan, "E-mail on Race Sparks a Furor at Harvard Law: Student Regrets Questioning the Intelligence of Blacks"; Sacks and Thiel, *The Diversity Myth: Multiculturalism and Political Intolerance on Campus*.

7 McGowan, *Coloring the News: How Crusading for Diversity Has Corrupted American Journalism*.

all institutions must base their operations on rationalized and supposedly neutral bureaucratic and commercial standards. The result is suppression of habits and attitudes that tie people together and enable them to form complex common goals and get work done pleasantly, efficiently, and cooperatively. Instead of relying on informal perceptions and understandings, which would inevitably reflect particular cultural patterns, employees undergo thought reform and parrot "corporate visions" everyone must pretend to embrace enthusiastically.[8] To make matters worse, affirmative action creates factions within every organization that depend for their position on victim status. The result is replacement of mutual trust by institutionalized suspicion, defensiveness, and rancor.

Not surprisingly, the destruction of the authority of particular culture bears especially heavily on cultural institutions. Rather than presenting, defending, and developing a particular culture, which is likely to be one traditionally dominant at least locally, they must subvert it. Anything else would make them agents of oppression. Traditional and high cultures thus turn against themselves. They lose their specific function in the ordering of the life of a people and, to the extent to which they are not replaced by commercial pop culture, become hobbies, theaters of careerism, markers of status, or instruments of subversion.

Public Spirit

More generally, inclusiveness suppresses public spirit. It wants to equalize the rewards of social life for different sorts of people and, to this end, insists on separating the functional aspects of social life from religion, lifestyle, and ethnicity, and so from any specific community setting. The result is that public spirit loses its natural home.

Public spirit ties public to private concerns. It depends on common understandings of personal obligations and the public good, and thus on shared goals, understandings, and expectations. Such

---

8 For the nature of corporate "diversity training," see Horowitz, *The Authoritarian Roots of Corporate Diversity Training: Jane Elliott's Captive Eyes and Minds.*

understandings arise naturally, if people connect on grounds of community affiliation and thus in a way that implicates religion, lifestyle, and ethnicity. For this reason, public spirit is most at home in a society that is religiously and culturally coherent.[9]

It can also exist in a more diverse society, but is more likely to do so, if the groups of which the society is composed can make their own contributions in their own way. This requires freedom of self-organization. Both WASP and Jewish organizations were long noted for civic involvement, but their interests, perspectives, and ways of doing things differed, so that they maintained their involvement in somewhat different styles and with somewhat different objects. Organizations that are identifiably one or the other have therefore been more likely than more inclusive organizations to have a view of the world and their place in it that is coherent enough to support common action for public ends.

If shared understandings weaken, as they do, if private organizations are not allowed to choose members in accordance with felt affinities, trust dwindles, common feeling dissipates, and material success becomes divorced from shared loyalties and understandings of the use to be made of it. Organizational and public life thus lose their moral aspects and become more and more an arena of ambition, greed, and manipulation. Any residual altruism is likely to be sentimental, abstract, and ineffectual. It is no accident that the revolutions of the '60s and reforms of the '70s led to "the decade of greed" in the '80s and the "me generation" forever after. In the absence of *noblesse oblige*,[10] participation in public affairs becomes ideological, self-seeking, or weak and sporadic. The sole remaining public ideal, equality, becomes

9 Ethnic diversity injures social trust, not only between but within ethnic groups. Putnam, "E Pluribus Unum: Diversity and Community in the Twenty-first Century."

10 The very concept of *noblesse oblige* is at odds with that of democratic citizenship: "Indeed you can usually tell when the concepts of democracy and citizenship are weakening. There is an increase in the role of charity and in the worship of volunteerism. These represent the élite citizen's imitation of *noblesse oblige*; that is, of pretending to be aristocrats or oligarchs, as opposed to being citizens." Saul, *Reflections of a Siamese Twin: Canada at the End of the Twentieth Century.*

a racket in which the discontented are bought off by giving a few of their representatives positions of wealth and power. If Obama is president and Oprah is a billionaire, then black people have made progress, even if 72 percent of black children are illegitimate, one in eight young black men is in prison, and the Congressional Black Caucus is shot through with corruption.[11]

Suppression of Discussion

Inclusiveness is intrinsically at odds with free thought and discussion. Questioning it puts equal standing in doubt and thereby destroys it, so skepticism is considered oppressive in itself.[12] In addition, free inquiry based on normal intellectual standards reveals stubborn human differences and points to politically incorrect conclusions regarding them.

Extremism, Lying, and Abuse

It is common at all times for those who dissent from established views on basic points to be rejected, ridiculed, and ignored, but the extreme vehemence of the response with regard to inclusiveness and the inability or unwillingness of those attacked to defend themselves deserve special comment.

One reason for the violence of the reaction is the liberal and modern emphasis on reason, which results in the necessity of perverting it, in order to maintain the stability of social understandings. It is very difficult for liberal public discussion to reject and suppress the clear indications of science and scholarship, but inclusiveness must do so in order to deny the stubborn differences among groups. It is a situation that must somehow be resolved, and the method adopted is to redefine reason and reality to comply with the demands of inclusiveness and stomp on anyone who notices there is a problem.

11 See Lipton and Lichtblau, "In Black Caucus, a Fund-Raising Powerhouse." Also see 'Blacks,' pp. 122 ff. below.

12 See Waldron, *The Harm in Hate Speech (Oliver Wendell Holmes Lectures, 2009)*, for arguments in favor of banning speech that deprives the vulnerable of assurance their equal dignity will be respected.

All inquiry treated as legitimate must yield politically acceptable results, and the process that arrived at them has to be presented as unquestionably free and rational. The result is corruption of biology, sociology, and psychology, as well as political and ethical thought. Science and scholarship become distorted,[13] journalism tendentious, and education propagandistic. The obvious must be ignored or treated as inconceivable, so that the world becomes incomprehensible. Journalists express bafflement over homegrown Islamic terrorism every time it occurs,[14] and the lesser success of blacks and women startles people and provokes the same debunked explanations every time it comes to notice.[15]

Other factors are also at work. One of them is the artificiality of discussions related to inclusiveness, which makes natural reactions of ordinary people disruptive to the point of vandalism, as if someone blurted out that the king has no clothes in a country where the penalty for public nudity is death. Under such circumstances, people have no idea how to go about defending themselves when they say the obvious.

Another is the energy and enthusiasm of the attackers. Some of them have a direct personal stake in inclusiveness, others are motivated by the moral and intellectual superiority correct positions confer, still others by the pleasure of licensed abuse of dissenters in a world grown terminally sensitive, caring, and dull. Much of the energy is due to the joy of scapegoating.[16] The assumption that doubts regarding inclusivist dogma demonstrate hatred shows that private reactions to diversity issues are often grossly incorrect. People stubbornly feel more tied to some groups than to others. They believe that a Jew is more likely to be a competent lawyer than a black man. And they notice unpleasant things about some groups that they are forbidden to see. The

13 Mangan, "The Persecution of Politically Incorrect Scientists."

14 Serwer, "How to Profile a Terrorist."; Auster, "Non-Islam Theories of Islamic Extremism"; Auster, "Refusing to Say That Muslim Terrorists Are Muslims."

15 Hoste, "Smart People Playing Dumb."

16 For a discussion of the role of scapegoating within progressive modernity, see Bertonneau, "The Apocalypse of Modernity."

result is that they feel permanently in the wrong on points that are now accepted as fundamental. The practical solution is to deny the evidence of their senses (the king's clothes are indeed beautiful!) and expunge their own perceptions and reactions by attributing them to the demonized other, to the "racist" and "bigot."

Conservatives, less ideological and more concrete in their thinking than liberals, but no less attached to accepted ways of thinking, try to maintain the no-differences orthodoxy without following through on its logic in as many respects. That, of course, lays them open to the accusation that they do not really believe the orthodoxy. When put to the question and called upon to explain themselves, they cannot do so coherently, since they are trying to deal with realities through an orthodoxy that denies them. Their own principles convict them, and all they can do is abase themselves and try to buy forgiveness, while realizing that they do not deserve it.[17]

Permissible Dissent

Discussion of human differences is nonetheless permitted to some extent, when the effect is to disrupt traditional understandings or otherwise advance inclusiveness. For example, there is some freedom to discuss sex differences, as long as the conclusion is that they make no practical difference, show women to be better, or point to something that should be done for them. Cultural and religious differences can also be discussed, when the effect is to promote liberal modernity. One can denounce Christianity, religion in general, and "fundamentalism" (religion that is not simply poeticized liberalism) in the most ignorant and bigoted terms. And one can assert the superiority of distant, past, minority, or invented religious and cultural traditions. On the other hand, criticism of Judaism is viewed as anti-Semitic in tendency and criticism of Islam as "Islamophobic" and even "racist." The latter, at least, has sometimes been subjected to criminal penalties in Western countries.

---

17 Something of the sort seems part of the explanation for Summers' and Watson's behavior, as well as that of politicians such as Trent Lott.

Racial differences are basically beyond discussion, at least by white people.[18] This special position is not altogether arbitrary. Unlike culture and religion, biological race has no intellectual content and, unlike sex, it lacks a natural function that gives rise to a system of cooperation among complementary opposites. For that reason, given the modern tendency to view conflict as basic to human relations, any recognition of racial differences, or even recognition of the legitimacy of race as a category, is thought to lead directly to radical existential conflict that can end only in a Final Solution.

Destruction of Thought

It would not be so easy to suppress discussion in the supposed citadels of Western rationality, if it were not ready to be suppressed. The incompatibility of science and inclusivist liberalism, together with their joint necessity for the current regime, suggests that fundamental inconsistencies in the modern outlook are leading to radical disorders in thought as such.

Liberalism, Scientism, and Dogma

In some ways it seems odd that liberals should suppress discussion of human differences and other difficult topics. After all, they believe in science and rationality, and science and rationality tell us men and groups differ. Why not face up to the situation? Whether the goal is equality or anything else, we are more likely to realize it, if we understand and deal with the world as it is. Or so it would seem.

The problem is that liberalism and scientism are more than predilections for freedom and modern natural science. Together they make up a system of understandings that now has supreme public authority. For this reason, people look to them for answers to life's basic questions. They must function as a religion, and this

---

18 It has nonetheless been possible recently to discuss the hypothesis that European anti-Semitism has ended by making Ashkenazi Jews more intelligent. Cochran, Hardy, and Harpending, "Natural History of Ashkenazi Intelligence."

means that they make certain demands on the world. A religion of sin and redemption makes no sense in a world of perpetual this-worldly progress. In the same way, a utopian scheme of thought makes no sense, if the world resists human wishes in basic ways. It must insist that the world is such that utopia can be realized and, indeed, that the goals of the utopia are the highest goals possible.

Liberalism tells us that our rational goals in acting are autonomy and preference satisfaction, that is to say, living by our own rules and getting what we want. It must nonetheless function as a principle of government, so it must give people reason to accept its authority. Its absolute preference for self-realization over self-sacrifice would justify resentment, resistance, and rebellion by those who have enduring reason for dissatisfaction. For this reason, liberalism must assure people that they will get along, if they go along. In particular, it cannot admit that there are irremediable inequalities and evils. Nor can it accept that there are intractable differences in human qualities like intelligence. It is based on a vision of human autonomy, the ability to decide for ourselves what we will be. If some are stubbornly different from others in ways no one would choose, autonomy is a mirage and liberalism makes no sense. Such a result is obviously unacceptable to liberals.

The problem is exacerbated by the modern tendency to treat human life as part of nature, with nature understood as a blind network of material causation. This tendency is at odds with the liberal vision of human autonomy, so it introduces a fundamental inconsistency into liberal modernity that makes rational discussion of human life impossible. It also leads to a tendency to deny natural harmonies and to treat conflict as the basic social reality. Those who accept scientism and admit the reality and significance of group differences are therefore likely to be tempted by genuine racism, the view that conflict among biological groups is the ultimate social reality. Hence the outrage among liberals in response to any suggestion that there are group differences that matter.

Science Wars

But is the attack on rationality specifically a liberal thing? Many people believe it is much more characteristic of the right. Some writers, for example, have complained about a conservative (or at least Republican) "war on science."[19] The complaint is not surprising. Liberalism is closely connected to scientism, and its adherents view opposition as intrinsically opposed to knowledge. From their standpoint, the right is anti-science by definition.

Nor is this view simply invented, since there is a conflict between the traditionalist and technological attitudes that sometimes leads to bad conduct by representatives of the opposing tendencies. Sometimes proponents of science claim more than is legitimate, and sometimes the tendency among conservatives to try to gain status and score points by mimicking their opponents' style of reasoning leads them to base arguments on obviously distorted versions of science (e.g. "creation science") instead of other forms of argument that would be more to the point.

However, the danger to science from the right is plainly exaggerated. The tendencies of liberal and scientific institutions line up with each other,[20] so rightists have very little power over science or science education.[21] When they win some disputed point, they are fighting the tide, and their victory will most likely be reversed in an election cycle or two. And, in any case, most such victories (as in the case of research involving embryonic stem cells) have to do with ethics rather than science as such. They relate to the position and authority of science as an institution rather than the principles and practice of science as an intellectual pursuit.

The liberal war on the integrity of science as a rational structure is far more comprehensive and effective, because it comes

---

19 Mooney, *The Republican War on Science*. Also see Dean, "At a Scientific Gathering, U.S. Policies Are Lamented."

20 Levin, "Science and the Left."

21 In contrast, consider then-Clinton White House policy adviser Elena Kagan's ability to get the American College of Obstetricians and Gynecologists to insert language she had drafted into a report on partial-birth abortion. Coffin, "Kagan's Abortion Distortion."

from within a related and allied stream of thought. It includes suppression of research on human differences, obvious misallocation of resources (as in the cases of AIDS funding[22] and initiatives to get more women in science),[23] pervasive interference with staffing and tenure decisions in the name of equal opportunity,[24] and retaliation against scientists for their political or social views,[25] or for scientific views thought to have political implications, going so far as to incite actual violence against sociobiologists and IQ researchers. At times, the liberal war on scientific integrity has even led to fraud by prominent scientists.[26]

The liberal war on science and rationality is also much less noticed than the so-called Republican war against the same. It is carried on to promote causes that all respected authorities, including leading scientists and scientific organizations, treat as

22 See *Estimates of Funding for Various Research, Condition, and Disease Categories (RCDC)*.

23 See Allen, "Science Quotas for Women–A White House Goal," on Obama administration plans to expand the antidiscrimination provisions of Title IX to women's participation in science, technology, engineering, and mathematics. Also see Ganga, "Berkeley High May Cut Lab Classes to Fund Programs for Struggling Students," regarding a proposal to cut spending on science instruction at Berkeley High School and use the money to try to close gaps in ethnic and racial achievement.

24 Munro, "Slotting Scientists: Higher-education Officials Are Trying to Boost Diversity in Science Departments Without Running Afoul of the Supreme Court."

25 Salter, "Professor Dumped from Oil Spill Team over Writings."

26 Wade, "Study Debunks Stephen Jay Gould's Claim of Racism on Morton Skulls." Human sexuality is a particularly fertile field for high-end scientific and scholarly malfeasance. See George, "'Shameless Acts' Revisited: Some Questions for Martha Nussbaum"; Finnis, "'Shameless Acts' in Colorado: Abuse of Scholarship in Constitutional Cases"; Bradley, "Academic Integrity Betrayed"; Reisman and Eichel, *Kinsey, Sex and Fraud: The Indoctrination of a People*; Freeman, *Margaret Mead in Samoa: The Making and Unmaking of an Anthropological Myth*. Also see Marks, "Same-sex Parenting and Children's Outcomes"; Regnerus, "How Different Are the Adult Children of Parents Who Have Same-sex Relationships? Findings from the New Family Structures Study"; Smith, "An Academic Auto-da-Fé"; Allen, Pakaluk, and Price, "Nontraditional Families and Childhood Progress Through School."

beyond question.[27] When Lawrence Summers and James Watson lost their positions for saying the wrong thing, they did not stand their ground and complain about their opponents' irrational and anti-scientific conduct. Instead, they confessed their own sinfulness and begged for forgiveness.

The End of Science?

In spite of the status of modern natural science in Western life and thought, academic leftists are generally skeptical of it, because they favor a postmodern outlook that puts distinctions and standards in doubt.[28] Since science depends on a stable structure of understandings, the influence of such attitudes among governing and intellectual elites may put the future of science in question.

Institutions do not last forever, and it is not clear why modern natural science should be different. There are strong motives for maintaining it, but there have been strong motives for maintaining many institutions that have vanished. Science cannot function outside a particular intellectual and social setting. There must, for example, be a public sphere in which discussion is free and truth valued without regard to tendency. That situation has not always existed, does not exist today to the extent it did in the recent past, and is not likely to last forever.

Postmodern tendencies have changed the intellectual setting in which science is carried on by debunking concepts of objectivity and truth. At a more practical and institutional level, science has come to depend on government and other large institutions. Pleasing officials has become the key to a successful scientific career, and officials usually prefer stability to the destabilizing effects of new knowledge. This preference will only grow, to the extent that international institutions make competition among states less of a factor. Historical periods defined by warring states have generally been much more creative than empires.

The greater the authority of science, the more important it is

---

27 See Pinker, *The Blank Slate: The Modern Denial of Human Nature.*

28 See Sokal and Bricmont, *Fashionable Nonsense: Postmodern Intellectuals' Abuse of Science*; Gross and Levitt, *Higher Superstition: The Academic Left and Its Quarrels with Science.*

to those in power to control what it says, and, the greater its success, the more likely it is to be captured by opportunists, time-servers, and the power-hungry. Since this is so, and since scientism denies transcendence and tends to identify truth with practical consequences, it is far from certain that scientists of the future will resist giving their superiors whatever they want.[29] Even today, leading popularizers of science are known for their political correctness, and scientists who fall short on this point, like James Watson, are quickly purged without protest.

The end of science as a coherent rational activity is therefore a possibility. That need not, however, mean the end of something called science, or of scientism. Scientism promotes postmodernism by denying essences and stable identities, and postmodernism discredits ordinary ways of thinking and so leads to an insistence on certified expertise that supports scientism. For now, scientism and postmodernism go together, and the two can exist independently of actual science.

The End of Thought?

The decline and corruption of modern natural science means trouble for Western thought in general. A variety of conditions, from trends in education to the state of the arts and political discussion, makes it appear that Western society is growing less able to think clearly and effectively.[30] The conviction of our ruling class that they are by far the most intelligent and enlightened people who ever lived is itself a sign of stupidity, or at least of ignorance and narcissism.

There are several reasons that might explain the trend. Some relate specifically to inclusiveness. I have discussed the corrupting effect, given the privileged position of neutral scientific investigation in today's thought, of the suppression of discussion and inquiry regarding human differences. In addition,

---

29 See Charlton, "The Story of Real Science."

30 The apparent collapse of Jewish academic achievement suggested by Unz, "The Myth of American Meritocracy," may be a sign of things to come. On more general trends, see Murray, *Human Accomplishment: The Pursuit of Excellence in the Arts and Sciences, 800 BC to 1950.*

• Thought depends on recognizing and applying patterns. Relating individual cases to patterns means discrimination and prejudice, so inclusiveness requires suppression of the habits of mind that make thought possible.[31]

• Thought also depends on intellectual standards, which are disfavored, because they make some people look bad. Diverse voices should not be suppressed, so supportiveness becomes the favored response to expression of all sorts, as long as the expression is consistent with the purposes of the liberal inclusivist regime.

• Inclusiveness also insists on supervised mechanical unity of unlike components, and productive thought and discussion can be neither supervised nor mechanical. Complex and subtle activities such as scholarly inquiry and speculative thought are aided by common histories, understandings, and commitments, as well as freedom of association, and inclusiveness intentionally disrupts such things. For this reason, it disrupts thought and discussion even regarding topics that appear to have nothing to do with it.

There are also broader features of modern life that tend to destroy the possibility of complex and coherent thought:

• The absorption of social functions by bureaucracy and commerce makes serious thought less important as a day-to-day matter for ordinary people. Consumer goods and social programs replace the art of living, which requires thought.

• Electronic diversions and propaganda train people out of the habit of consecutive reasoning. Tweets, texting, and multitasking mean discussion never comes to the point.

• The denial of the good, beautiful, and true in favor of rhetoric and power leads to the replacement of thought by politics, propaganda, and partisanship throughout intellectual life.

• Thought requires engagement with reality. Electronic entertainment, social constructivism, and the distance between

---

31 For a general discussion of the necessity of prejudice, see Dalrymple, *In Praise of Prejudice: The Necessity of Preconceived Ideas.*

cause and effect in a complex globalized society mean people do not engage reality and consider it theoretically impossible to do so.

- At a cruder level, less intelligent people have more children in today's world, and children take after their parents, so over time average intelligence declines.

On the other side of the ledger we have the increased availability of information, argument, and discussion on the Internet. This development is not likely to give a failing public order the principle of unity it needs to pull itself together. Nonetheless, it can help refugees from that order construct something better to live by, and this is very likely the most important intellectual work to be done today.

6

The Inclusivist Regime

The usual leftist claim is that established social and moral principles serve the interests of the ruling classes. The claim is not applied to principles of which the left approves, and in particular it is not applied to inclusiveness. This is unfortunate, because it is obvious that inclusiveness serves governing elites by eliminating competing authorities and justifying an elaborate system of irresponsible control by those at the top.

A New Ruling Class

Inclusiveness rejects and suppresses all non-liberal principles of authority. The rhetoric is familiar. Religious authority is bigoted and oppressive. Family authority is narrow, sexist, agist, ethnocentric, heterosexist, and intertwined with patriarchal religion. And authority based on history and tradition is exclusionary and racist. If you speak of Southern history, blacks do not like it. Meanwhile, the history of the American West is offensive to Mexicans and Indians, and New England history excludes Somalian immigrants, while including episodes that upset Quakers and Catholics. The only history that remains valid is the history that led to present-day liberalism. You can appeal to Western history and standards, if you want, but only if you identify "the West" with the advanced liberal order and its victory over all competitors.

The Managerial Perspective

When natural and traditional principles are rejected as ignorant, irrational, and hateful, then money, bureaucracy, and certified expertise become the sole permissible principles of social order.

The result is an enormous transfer of power to experts, verbalizers, and managers, leading to dominance by a particular class composed of people whose complementary functions and strategic role in social institutions give them a common outlook and interests. On the design side, the favored group includes legal experts, social scientists, and other theoreticians, and, on the implementation side, lawyers, jurists, journalists, educators, media people, business leaders, and civil servants.

General conditions of public life facilitate the consolidation of that class's power. The degree of government involvement in economic and social life today makes political issues infinitely complicated. There is too much spin and maneuvering for ordinary people to keep up with them, and, in any event, the people have been deprived of a literal or figurative common language. All the machinery of publicity tells them they should trust those who run things, even as they are bogged down in diversions and must attend to the ordinary concerns of life. The natural outcome of such conditions is an arrangement like the EU, in which experts and professional managers join together to run everything, leaving ordinary people out of the loop, except to provide a facade of democratic legitimacy and the occasional reality check. Representative institutions remain, but at the national level their hands are tied by treaties and directives, while at the transnational level, wherein the power increasingly lies, there is no minimally coherent people to hold them to account. And, in any case, the representatives are *ipso facto* members of the ruling class, who soon adopt ruling class standards and aspirations, if they did not hold them already.

The resulting state of affairs is considered non-oppressive, because it is based on neutral standards not beholden to any particular ethnic, cultural, or religious tradition. Control of education, scholarship, and mass communication enables ruling elites to establish support for the system as an unquestionable orthodoxy and define dissenters who favor traditional authorities and forms of social organization as bigots. Under such circumstances, suppressing alternative principles and authorities comes to seem a simple matter of suppressing oppressive irrationalities.

From the standpoint of those at the top, everything is as it should be. Our ruling class does not see their position as a matter of political or personal advantage, but as a requirement of reason itself. Professionals should manage and they should answer to each other rather than to the ignorant, self-interested, and bigoted many. After all, to be professional is to be expert and by definition to know better. Legitimate disagreement with management by experts is impossible, since it is experts who tell us what counts as legitimate, what views make sense, and how disagreements should be resolved. Inherited and traditional institutions are irrational and unjust, so they have to be done away with.

To give up their ideal of a rationalized global order based on the categories that make sense to professional managers, our governing classes would have to abandon their class interests, their understanding of rationality and justice, and their understanding of who they are as human beings. A professor in a prestigious university or a partner in a Wall Street law firm does not have the special position he does because he is white or American or Episcopalian or a New Yorker or a man rather than a woman. He has it, because he is part of a professional class that is entitled to rule the world, and as such is in a position to look down on people who think traditional distinctions matter. Are our rulers liberal? Do they believe in inclusiveness? One might as well ask if Louis XIV was a monarchist.

Suppression of Dissidence

In any event, there is no one in a position to object effectively. The absorption of thought, study, and the arts by academic and cultural bureaucracies that are integral parts of the regime makes serious independent thought difficult. Also, their situation in life turns intelligent and industrious people into unimaginative functionaries totally absorbed in their social position. The institutions now dominant are competitive and meritocratic, within the limits of ethnic and other preferences, and the work is demanding, so that those who get to the top get there by giving themselves wholly to the commitments and ways of thought that inspire their employers. Their education, their social setting and identity, the conditions of their working lives, and their absorption in career and consumption allow little scope or basis for independence.[1]

Nor are the people in a position to resist. Without an independent structure of discussion and authority, they cannot organize themselves effectively. The destruction of non-liberal authorities and forms of order[2] enables the regime to maintain itself with the appearance of consent and minimal use of force. The people have the theoretical power to end affirmative action, mass third-world immigration, and other inclusivist initiatives, but they let them stand. Thus, these measures are held to have democratic legitimacy in spite of their unpopularity. If the people act to assert themselves, those in power can give them something and then outwait them, while taking steps to reverse practical consequences and prevent repetition. The expansion of the EU, in which referenda are repeated and legal forms varied, until the right result is reached, is another case in point.

Beyond that, objections to the indefinite extension of the liberal regime are excluded as advocacy of oppression. They are a kind of hate speech, since, at least implicitly, they favor freedom to discriminate.[3] The position of the powers that be is thus put

1 The inclusivist regime tends to suppress thought in any event. See 'Destruction of Thought,' pp. 87 ff. above.

2 A particularly clear example of that tendency is the reduction by the Obama administration of "freedom of religion," which allows an important role for religion in public life, to "freedom of worship," understood as a branch of the right of privacy.

3 Article 4 of the International Convention on the Elimination of All Forms of Racial Discrimination requires parties to "declare an offence punishable by law all dissemination of ideas based on racial superiority [and] incitement to racial discrimination," defined to include

any distinction, exclusion, restriction or preference based on race, colour, descent, or national or ethnic origin which has the . . . effect of . . . impairing the . . . enjoyment or exercise, on an equal footing, of human rights and fundamental freedoms in the political, economic, social, cultural or any other field of public life.

Under this provision, it may well be criminal to propose to get rid of racial affirmative action on the grounds that groups differ in average capability. Claims that racial groups differ in average capability are evidently claims of racial superiority, and proposing to allow people to discriminate in employment based on something racially linked opens the door to impairing the enjoyment on an equal footing of the fundamental right to work.

beyond criticism. Democracy extends only to those who accept basic democratic principles such as equality and tolerance, so the views of the non-inclusive do not count. The bigot is the new faggot, the man defined by his attachment to a way of life radically at odds with basic principles of legitimate social organization. The result is a supposedly democratic regime in which the views of most actual people on basic issues like immigration, affirmative action, and the place of religion in public life are excluded as illegitimate and irrelevant.

So it is not possible, even in concept, to object to the present state of affairs, except on the grounds that it does not go far enough. Those who object to elite rule and the general tendency of events are ignorant losers who want to impose their prejudices on others. "Tea partiers," who offend through inchoate opposition to big government, are considered racist know-nothings and treated as legitimate objects of obscene sexual abuse by reputable news organizations.[4] If dissidents manage to win something through the democratic process, this is a flaw in the process that judges and administrators should rectify in whatever way seems most effective.[5] The more of them there are, the more important it is to keep them cowed and to re-educate their children.

Daily Life

What is it like to live in a modern, diverse, vibrant, tolerant, inclusive, multicultural society? Everyday experience in early

---

4 CNN and MSNBC routinely referred to them as "teabaggers" (for definition, see "Urban Dictionary: Definition of 'tea bagger'"), with suggestive logos and double entendre-laden monologues to match.

5 See Romer v. Evans, 517 U.S. 620 (1996), which invalidated Proposition 2, an attempt to keep Colorado localities from making homosexuals a protected class for purposes of antidiscrimination laws; "CA's Anti-Immigrant Proposition 187 Is Voided, Ending State's Five-Year Battle with ACLU, Rights Groups," for events leading to abandonment of Proposition 187, which tried to keep illegal aliens from using health care, public education, and other social services in California; and Mac Donald, "Elites to Anti-Affirmative-Action Voters: Drop Dead," for the administrative sabotage of Proposition 209, which banned affirmative action in California.

twenty-first century America allows us to sketch major tendencies in bold strokes.

Growing Up Absurd

Such a society lacks sustaining stories, symbols, and models of a good life, and, indeed, intentionally eradicates them. Such things are racist, since they reflect the specifics of a particular culture, and sexist and heteronormative, since they express fundamental patterns of human life. They are also theocratic, since they connect the order of human life to a particular understanding of the order of the world.

They must therefore be suppressed. The result is that life, culture, and human relations become crude, rude, perverse, willful, violent, and boring. Abolishing recognized patterns of a good life consigns people more and more to impulse, dissipation, and boredom, or to the tyranny of the cruder motives: lust, envy, greed, hate, ambition.[6] Sentimental altruism, personal attachments, memories of traditional order, and the advantages of pleasing others provide some leavening, but, without concrete images of order, there is nothing reliable to bring immediate impulse into a humane system.

In such a society, which lacks objective standards of character, human personality comes to base itself on narcissistic self-affirmation that masks depression and emotional fragility.[7] Young people deprived of culture invent their own based on commercial pop culture. They live in a world populated by jocks, nerds, wimps, players, hipsters, couch potatoes, and other trivial types. Those who reject such identifications define themselves by reference to "alternative" culture, an attempt to negate the trivial that lacks substantive content and has no way to rise above what it rejects.

They never grow up. How could they, where there is nothing to grow into and no serious responsibilities to give adult activities

---

6 A further result is a decline in empathy. How would people without close personal ties learn to feel it? See Konrath, O'Brien, and Hsing, "Changes in Dispositional Empathy in American College Students over Time."

7 Lazartigues et al., "New society, new families: a new basic personality? From the neurotic to the narcissistic-hedonistic personality."

weight? Education disintegrates for inability to treat one thing as better than another. Marriage and family cannot provide a pattern of life among people who recognize no settled connections, idealize self-creation, and view practical necessities as the responsibility of either the individual or the state. So young people do not get married, or, if they do, their marriages are fragile, sterile, or both. Without a pattern to aspire to, the relation between the sexes sinks into low-level war: hos and playahs at the lower levels, game[8] and the New Girl Order[9] at the higher. Refugees from the conflict swell the ranks of homosexuals, porn fans, video game addicts, feminists, misogynists, and the new sexless.

Children are badly brought up, never born at all, or brought up to be winners in a competitive game of careers and consumption.[10] Foreign workers are imported to take the place of the missing and nonfunctional. Their presence and numbers further disintegrate weakened local cultures, while their absence from their native homeland disrupts their own.[11] Those who assimilate soon reproduce the problems of the native population. Those who do not sink to the level of a hereditary uncultured proletariat.[12]

The older generation, who after all created or at least accepted the situation, are no better. They have gotten along by going along and soon enough accommodate themselves to whatever comes up. Most often, they accept it as good and take advantage of what it offers.[13]

A World Without Independent Standards

Under such conditions no one knows who he is, so no one knows

8 Techniques for manipulating women to bed them. See Heartiste, "Chateau Heartiste: Where Pretty Lies Perish."

9 Female careerists who choose high-end consumption over family responsibilities and connections to men. Hymowitz, "The New Girl Order."

10 Recent claims that upbringing does not matter (see Caplan, "Good News and Bad News on Parenting") are really claims that it is society in general and not our parents in particular who bring us up. Such claims underline the importance of general social conditions.

11 See 'Hispanics,' pp. 125 ff. below.

12 Frum, "Ending Illegal Immigration Benefits Economy–CNN.com."

13 "STDs Running Rampant In Retirement Community: Doctor Blames Viagra, Lack Of Sex Education"; Madeleine Scinto, "Randy Grands Take over Online Realm - Number of Seniors Playing the Field More Than Doubles."

how to speak or act. Personal identity disintegrates and, with it, the possibility of self-rule. Manners become careless and awkward, conversation shot through with "likes" and "whatevers," and standards of conduct (other than political correctness) vague to the point of uselessness.

The fluidity of relationships does away with conventions and common understandings based on extended common experience of life. There is no answerability and no basis for loyalty or penalty for cutting corners. Intelligent public life is replaced by suspicion, corruption, inefficiency, irrationality, and mindless dogma. All is slogan, spin, propaganda and bullying, with certified experts trying to take charge of an increasingly nonfunctional social order in the name of their own version of rationality.

Normal spontaneous responses are silenced, because they involve prejudgment and prejudice. Spontaneity needs a background of assumed normality, and the normal has been abolished. Pretense and moral posturing become the norm. If you want acceptance, you have to pretend that your responses are other than they are and the world is something other than what it evidently is. The only escape from pretense is crude willfulness, and there is plenty of that as well. No one has an assured place, so there is always something to prove. If you are not a psychopath able to invent a persona and impose it on others, you are defined by your relation to a public order based on formal institutions, abstractions, and whim. You are your bank balance, job title, and consumption choices. Ambition becomes unrewarding, but to give it up, in the absence of stable higher goals, is to sink into the stupor, self-indulgence, resentment, and brutality of a growing class of proles.[14]

The arts reflect the new public order. Architecture becomes inhuman and disorienting,[15] literature self-involved or sensationalist. The performing arts sink into commercial junk for the masses, official state-subsidized high culture for the classes, and

---

14 See Dalrymple, *Life at the Bottom*. It is worth noting that the way of life of the upper classes also deteriorates, but not as much, so they gain a relative advantage.

15 See Salingaros, *Anti-Architecture and Deconstruction*.

various alternative expressions that show dissatisfaction with what is on offer, but lack a positive vision. The arts that claim to be serious favor the regime that provides their environment, audience, and patrons, while pretending to a radically critical stance that in substance mostly consists of attacks on the regime's opponents.

The New Hypocrisy

In the background, of course, life goes on. People have no principled way to oppose the regime, but piece together an order to live by, however they can. They go to church and get married, do their best for their children, friends, and neighbors, and are often much better than their stated principles. If nothing else, they try to be "nice." Even in the arts, a great deal of good work goes on, mostly in the background and at the lower levels, springing out of a natural love for what is good that remains in spite of the absence of theoretical justification.

The contrast between practice and official theory becomes especially stark in the social strata where ambition checks self-indulgence and intelligence points out practical problems with official ideals. The educated upper class keep their lives in order for the sake of their careers and those of their children. They decline to live by the moral libertarianism they have made normative for society as a whole through the demands of tolerance and the reign of neutral managerial expertise. That is for the lower classes, who rely on the common understandings in their surroundings more than the demands of a chosen career path and who are allowed no culture that corresponds to their conditions of life. Profound differences have therefore appeared between social classes in such indicia of well-being as marital stability, care for children, economic productivity, and even church-going.[16] Inclusiveness may or may not make the rich richer, but it assuredly makes the poor poorer by depriving them of goods money cannot buy and eventually of the qualities that make effective action possible.[17]

16 Murray, *Coming Apart: The State of White America,* 1960–2010; Brooks, "The Opportunity Gap."

17 For an indication of what that can mean, see Dalrymple, *Life at the Bottom.*

Multicultural Culture

The antidiscrimination principle forbids any particular culture to be authoritative, since this would discriminate against those with a different cultural background. The logical effect is the abolition of culture as such. What cannot be public and authoritative is not culture, but private habit and taste.

Multicultural Particularities

Nonetheless, no human group can function without common habits and understandings that its members are entitled to rely on. Like anything else, multicultural society must insist on its own particularities to exist at all. It thus has its own culture, one that trumps and suppresses the particular inherited cultures it claims to respect.[18] This culture follows the lead of the institutions that are dominant, so it makes bureaucratic and commercial institutions uniquely authoritative. Careerism and consumerism become the guide for living, management and therapy the standard for human relations, and scientism the theory of publicly valid knowledge.

Such principles do not deal with all aspects of human life and, in particular, leave out love, loyalty, and the consequences of human weakness and the passage of time—failure, aging, death, and the succession of generations. The result is a culture that seems satisfactory mostly to those who expect to gain by the established order, who have experienced little and suffered few reverses, and whose main concerns relate to career, consumption, and the diversions of the moment.[19] Since it treats career and consumption as the human good and suppresses the habits, attitudes, and institutions that order and give dignity to the lives of ordinary people dealing with ordinary human problems, it is most satisfactory to hipsters and yuppies, and to upwardly-

18 Some diversity promoters say as much. They speak of a culture of inclusion, or call America a universal nation whose particularity it is to be universal.

19 See Twenge, Freeman, and Campbell, "Generational Differences in Young Adults' Life Goals, Concern for Others, and Civic Orientation, 1966–2009."

bound youth who hope to do well and expect their knowledge and perceptiveness to give them an advantage as competitive consumers.

Young people like to attach themselves to power that believes in itself. Inclusiveness makes them independent of their families and local communities. It enables them to identify with what is viewed as strongest, freest, most active, and most universal. It declares that they are winners who can take on anything. And it ignores distinctions the meaning of which it takes experience to understand. How could they possibly reject it? If they are told they should form themselves on its model, why would they do otherwise?

Identity

They may eventually have reason to regret their choice. Even for yuppies, hipsters, and careerists, multicultural culture leaves out too many aspects of human life to be satisfactory for long. To quote one of the most poignant lines in Western literature, *Sunt lacrimae rerum, et mentem mortalia tangunt*, which might be translated "We live in a vale of tears and the burden of our humanity touches us to our inmost depths."[20] To put it more prosaically, life eventually brings conflicts, slights, defeats, and losses, and the current succession of "me" generations has no way to deal with them.[21]

The deficiencies of multicultural culture are highlighted in connection with understandings of personal identity. Inclusiveness tells us that characteristics that traditionally define identity have no legitimate public role. If my specific identity—as a man, a member of a particular people, or whatever—affects my position in the world, then it is considered that I am being treated unequally because of who I am. To say that what I am should have no effect on my social position, however, is to say that I

20 Virgil, *Aeneid*.

21 For studies of the moral world of today's young adults, see Smith et al., *Lost in Transition: The Dark Side of Emerging Adulthood*; Twenge, *Generation Me: Why Today's Young Americans Are More Confident, Assertive, Entitled—and More Miserable Than Ever Before*.

should have no essential connection to the social order of which I am part and thus to estrange me from that order. The progress of inclusiveness is therefore the progress of alienation.[22]

Since man is social, depriving identity of a public role deprives it of its function even in private life. Loss of settled connections makes it impossible for multicultural man to identify anything very firmly. To make all identities equal is to keep them from making a difference. Everything dissolves in a haze of interchangeable possibilities, none of which matter much. Since identities do nothing to define our place in the world, they do not identify us in any significant way and are hardly identities at all. Under such circumstances, people lose character and become weak, conformist, trivial-minded, and easily manipulated. To make every individual sovereign, it turns out, is to cause him to vanish for lack of anything definite he can be.

Substitute Identities

That situation cannot last. We need to know who we are, so that we can place ourselves and understand how to act. What forms of identity are available, though? Progressives want man to be autonomous and invent his own, but it is not clear what that would mean. If I invent my identity, who is the "I" that invents it? Also, how does an identity I invent for myself become my identity? How does it identify me? If I decide I am Napoleon, does that make me Napoleon? If so, what does "Napoleon" mean?

Self-invention has its questionable side in any event. Fluidity of identity mostly benefits those adept at varying their self-presentation for their own purposes and getting others to accept the result, in other words, the manipulative and delusional. In a free-floating, postmodern world, the con man and psychopath accordingly become major social types.[23] Luckily, few people can simply

22 This situation has political effects: a man becomes one thing and society quite another, with no intrinsic connection between the two. Under such circumstances, normal grounds for loyalty disappear, and the individual's relation to the political order becomes basically a matter of self-interest.

23 See Malcolm, "Oh-oh! Politicians Share Personality Traits with Serial Killers: Study."

make up who they are, so, as always, most people's identities will be linked to their relationship to the social order and the goods it recognizes. We are social beings, so we identify ourselves by our social position. Suppressing traditional identities by insisting that they be interchangeable pushes new forms of identity to the fore that are based on permissible distinctions and thus able to function. For this reason, career, consumption, certified qualifications, and political correctness are at the heart of multicultural identity. I shop, therefore I am. I am who I am because I went to this college, work in this job, and live that lifestyle. Instead of the Catholic husband and father, we get the politically-correct careerist and consumer, instead of European culture, we get "Stuff White People Like."[24]

The new forms of identity inevitably correspond to new hierarchies of consideration and forms of exclusion, so that, from the standpoint of equality, it is not clear what has been gained. Also, the new identities have certain disadvantages. They are external and easily lost, and, for that reason, make people insecure, subservient, and devious. They tend to be content-free and purely comparative, so that what one gains from his identity others lose. And they deaden the imagination, because they relate to an absolutely quotidian world. Who needs them? The system is pointless, so people try to escape it. This is why the rebel without a cause has become a major social type, although not one whose efforts go anywhere. He is even a failure at rebelling: how can you rebel against liberation? In the end, people turn to anything at all as a way of establishing who they are, even defacing their own bodies through piercing, tattooing, cutting, or anorexia.

Coolness

Something more is needed, something that ties the man and his life to some principle that transcends particular needs and desires and makes them part of something larger and open-ended. One answer to this problem is support for the liberal order itself. To

---

24 That is, lifestyle accessories favored by affluent educated young whites. See Lander, *Stuff White People Like: A Definitive Guide to the Unique Taste of Millions.*

give your support to the official views and have correct attitudes on political, social, and moral issues is to identify yourself with the highest socially recognized standards and so give your life a significance beyond itself. Liberal social views have therefore become part of yuppie and hipster identity.

Problems remain, however. The liberal order is irretrievably prosaic and boring. It turns everything into a productive resource or consumption good and so effaces distinction and individuality. Its ideals are unsustaining, and it has no room for the soul. A makeshift remedy, but the best available within the liberal order, is provided by "coolness." It seems trivial, but people take it much more seriously than they admit. After all, what else is there?

Coolness started with jazz musicians and still has something of the spirit of the night, of escape from everyday reality, of unconditioned freedom, of improvisation without a goal. It is the liberal equivalent of the divine grace that bloweth where it listeth and none can define.[25] It has something in common with sanctity, inasmuch as the cool are in the world but not of it. They possess a certain disengagement, so that they are independent of their surroundings and not easily flustered or excited. They are not conventional and have a sort of perfect pitch in matters of perception, expression, and practical decision.

Of course, coolness is also very different from sanctity. Sanctity is about eternity, coolness about now. It has religious aspirations, but its hedonism and individualism mean they go nowhere. The lives of the saints have enduring interest, because they point to something beyond themselves. The lives of the hipsters do not. This lack of substantive content allows coolness a place in the spiritual world of liberalism, but is otherwise a radical defect. Coolness makes things a matter of style, which is why a clumsy attempt to be a saint is admirable, while a clumsy attempt to be cool is ridiculous. This also means that coolness cannot maintain standards. Miles Davis is dead, hipsters have gone mass-market, and grade-school children now have as much right to be cool as anyone.

At bottom, coolness is as silly as people think. It is notoriously

25 John 3:8.

unsustaining. Those who live by it either crash and burn, fall into gross hypocrisy ("sell out"), or grow out of it. Within the liberal order, though, growing out of it means growing out of the only thing, other than sex, drugs, celebrity, or lots and lots of money, that redeems life from quotidian dullness. It means turning into a boring, conventional, older person, just like Mom and Dad.

The Soul of Man Under Liberalism

The problem, then, with cultural accommodations to liberalism is that in the end none of them work. The problems it creates go too deep to live with in the long run. Inclusiveness functions as a religion, but it functions badly as such. Religion must define man's place in the world, and the modern outlook from which inclusiveness derives cannot do so coherently.

The problem is basic. The modern outlook insists on unitary theories that put everything on the same level, so that it tries to dissolve the individual into the world or the world into the individual. Neither makes sense, so moderns, including liberals, oscillate between the two. At bottom, liberalism wants to view the individual person as the Cartesian ego, a disembodied subject with no qualities other than the ability to have experiences and make choices. If we accept this understanding and view the external world from the radically subjective standpoint that results, it becomes something we construct from our sensations for the sake of our goals. Such an understanding affects our attitude toward our environment. It makes every particular tie to things outside ourselves seem an intrusion that has somehow gotten hold of us and is dragging us down.[26] The result is a compulsion to destroy attachments that make claims on us. Hence the insistence on sexual liberation, abolition of social roles, mass

---

26 Peggy Noonan, a writer who passes as conservative, tells us that American patriotism is "felt and spoken love for and fidelity to the ideas and ideals our country represents and was invented to advance—freedom, equality, pluralism." In contrast, a patriotism based on particular attachments amounts to a statement that "our mud is better than the other guy's mud." Noonan, "Failures of Imagination."

third-world immigration, multiculturalism, and so on. Society must be destroyed as a network of particular persons and relationships in a particular setting and turned into an abstract, neutral scheme for the satisfaction of desire.

The matter cannot rest there, because the Cartesian ego is so odd, philosophically. It is not part of the world of experience, and it is unclear how something with no positive qualities could be embodied. The result is a radical disconnection between self and world. Am I the only reality, because the subjective outlook is so privileged, or am I not real at all, because I have no enduring tangible qualities or connections? With respect to ourselves, such difficulties lead to insecurity, narcissism, and identity crises. With respect to our fellows, they lead to an obsession with the non-Western other.

Non-Westerners are not expected to understand themselves as free-floating Cartesian egos. Since they are not expected to view themselves this way, they can be seen as embodied and part of the world of experience without violating their presumed self-understanding. This gives them a very special, though ambiguous, significance. From one perspective, the Cartesian outlook turns Westerners into abstractions who hardly exist at all, while non-Westerners remain vibrant concrete realities. From another, it makes non-Westerners a colorful background, part of the Stuff White People Like, that accessorizes the narcissistic lifestyles of white, liberal Cartesians. There is no way within the liberal outlook to choose between the two, so particular liberals flop back and forth depending on mood and circumstances.

The problem naturally takes a religious form. The absorption of traditional religion by inclusiveness reflects in part an effort to answer religious questions in a scientistic world. In such a world, God is unthinkable, so people fall back on themselves. Their desires and concerns are what they live by. Indeed, they are That Than Which No Greater Can Be Conceived. So why not treat them as divine?[27]

The problem is that a religion of radical self-centeredness does not satisfy. We need a moral and spiritual order beyond ourselves

---

27 The reference, of course, is to Anselm's ontological argument.

that enables us to place and orient ourselves and make sense of our situation. One possible solution that seems consistent with liberalism is horizontal transcendence, i.e., standing in awe before other people as ineffably and unclassifiably other, disclosing to us a reality that cannot be reduced to our own categories and purposes and imposing peremptory moral obligations on us through their needs and desires.

On such a view, those most radically other than ourselves and the Cartesian ego, namely, Third World peasants or whoever, become natural exemplars of the holy. However, the solution is unstable, because the non-Western other is obviously no more holy than we are. We can respect people's human dignity and good qualities, but it is silly to overlook whatever flaws and limitations they have or to take them more seriously than we take ourselves and those to whom we have a more immediate connection. And, in any event, they are not so radically other, since they are people like ourselves.

The natural resolution would be acceptance of a truly transcendent order, in which we and the other both find a place. Liberal modernity excludes that answer, so the outcome is a messy compromise between self-involvement and sentimentality about non-Westerners and people on the margins. Among self-involved, spiritual-but-not-religious women, for example, this compromise often takes the form of an interest in third-world-themed home decor, fashion accessories, and styles of cooking that are a fitting complement to a soft left political outlook.

7

Progress or Decline?

The established order reflects established beliefs about man and the world, so it has its defenders, and they make some points that are hard to deny. If racism, sexism, homophobia, and the like are ultimate moral horrors, then public life has decisively improved. And if career and consumption are the highest human goods, the attempt to fine-tune their apportionment to exclude the effect of disfavored factors makes sense.

How to Decide?

But are career and consumption really the best things? And are traditional discriminations so very bad or even, simply as such, bad at all? After all, they have always pervaded social life, and they are basic to enduring patterns of cooperation that operate outside commercial and bureaucratic channels. Not everyone wants to live in a society that is purely commercial and bureaucratic, nor in one that enforces permanent cultural revolution for the sake of an impossible ideal of doubtful human value.

People view such issues differently. Some find particular social institutions and the attitudes and standards that support them intolerably burdensome. Those who feel burdened may dream of getting rid of them or at least radically changing them or depriving them of authority, thinking these goals to be worth any cost. The point applies to all social arrangements, though, not just those targeted by inclusiveness. Some people would have been happier in Calvin's Geneva, others would have thrived as Vikings and are miserable today because of limited opportunities for adventure and pillage. Nobody pays much attention to radical Calvinists or would-be Vikings, since across the board the institutions and interests now dominant would be injured by the rule of the saints or rampant piracy. In contrast, complaints about institutions like family and religion that stand in the way of unrestricted rule by the burgeoning institutions of liberal modernity get privileged status. They trump attachments to traditional ways, which are based on principles that are at odds with those now dominant and are therefore considered retrograde and wrong.

It is always possible to dispute facts and what they mean. If the liberal order makes us narcissistic, maybe this is the result of a superior consciousness of our freedom and human worth. If it leads to broken homes, this could show it empowers us to leave bad relationships and embrace the future. In any event, people at the top buy into post-1960s moral beliefs more consistently than others, and these beliefs have injured them much less.[1] Concern with career and status does a lot to keep their lives in order. Maybe current problems could be greatly mitigated, if everyone got with the program and adopted the yuppie lifestyle.

So who is right and who is wrong?[2] To deal with the issue requires a view of human nature and flourishing, but the difficulty is which view to take. Ethicists, psychologists, and philosophers disagree among themselves and have their own professional biases, so we cannot solve the problem by asking the experts, even if we can identify them. Popular consensus might be an answer, but few stick with it when inconvenient, and it is not even clear where to look for it. Is it the consensus of the moment or over time? Both have disadvantages. Current opinion can be a transitory reflection of impulse and propaganda, while traditional understandings can be a tissue of injustices and obsolete perspectives. Each sometimes gives answers that seem wrong, so why take either as the standard?

---

1 See Murray, *Coming Apart: The State of White America, 1960–2010.*

2 Americans seem divided within themselves on the issue. They pride themselves on being more open and tolerant than their parents, but also think the country is getting worse morally and socially. Cohn, "21 Charts That Explain American Values Today."

The Liberal Solution

Liberalism claims to avoid the need to answer such questions. It says that each of us should develop his own view of what life is about and apply it in his own case, leaving others to do the same. Hence the ethical subjectivism that is now publicly compulsory. Questions of good and bad must be kept as private as possible, so that each can be free to make his own decisions on his own grounds.[3] This principle has been taken so far that in much of the West it can now be criminal to say that one religion or scheme of sexual practice is better than another.[4]

Thus, liberalism tells us that the most basic issues should not be decided publicly or on their merits. Instead, they should be dealt with through the principle of giving everybody whatever he wants, as much and as equally as possible. How to do so is a question for experts, so that the practical solution for troublesome issues is to let liberal functionaries decide them implicitly, as they administer social life in the name of freedom, equality, prosperity, and security. Staff the Supreme Court with graduates of Yale and Harvard Law School, whose background and affiliations make them independent of America's historic

---

3 As the Supreme Court has said, "At the heart of liberty is the right to define one's own concept of existence, of meaning, of the universe, and of the mystery of human life." Planned Parenthood of Southeastern Pa. v. Casey, 505 U.S. 833 (1992).

4 Thus, for example, a lecturer in Austria was recently fined for "denigration of religious beliefs of a legally recognized religion," because she said "Mohammed [who consummated one of his marriages when his bride was 9 years old] had a thing for little girls." Kern, A Black Day for Austria. And a sidewalk preacher in England who held up a sign calling for an end to homosexuality, lesbianism, and immorality (and had soil thrown at him and water poured over his head for his pains) was convicted of a public order offence, and the conviction was upheld on appeal. Savill, "Preacher's Conviction over Anti-gay Sign Upheld." More recently, another sidewalk preacher was arrested and charged with violating public order after he told a passer-by and a homosexual police community support officer that, as a Christian, he believed homosexuality was one of a number of sins that go against the word of God. MailOnline, "Christian Preacher on Hooligan Charge after Saying He Believes That Homosexuality Is a Sin."

white Protestant majority, staff the major media with their friends,[5] and let these people and people like them decide everything significant.

Its Deficiencies

In this way, liberals respond to the difficulty of decision by appealing to neutral technical expertise and by trying to reduce the number of decisions that must be made publicly and explicitly. The problem with this response is that basic issues cannot be avoided, and expertise knows less than it thinks.

Academic thought has the same weaknesses as academic art. It is hard to argue against, because it is well-organized and well-positioned, and its proponents refuse to recognize the legitimacy of objections from outsiders. However, it leaves out considerations that are important, but hard to articulate in terms experts can deal with as experts. The result is that expert judgments lose touch with reality, especially when dealing with complex and subtle aspects of human life. Education and architecture provide good examples. Experts adopt theories they find persuasive, but the result is that students do not learn and people hate the built environment. Nor are experts disinterested. They have an interest in the abolition of traditional arrangements that enable people to run their own affairs in their own way. Those arrangements leave professionals and their view of things out of the loop, so asking experts about them is like asking automobile manufacturers about public transportation. They know a great deal that is relevant, but they have their own occupational interests and point of view, so why trust their judgment?

In any case, the liberal order inevitably decides basic issues. In particular, it decides what the good life is, and treats it as the satisfaction of individual preferences within a system that offers the same to others. The description of liberalism as a matter of procedure and neutral expertise obfuscates the real situation and puts the liberal vision of the good life beyond discussion by denying such a thing exists. It is typical of liberalism to try to elude discussion in such a way. Neither the liberal version of the good

5 See Gavin, "Kagan's Journo Friends."

life nor the liberal claim to combine maximum freedom with maximum efficiency, equality, and stability will bear looking into. Liberalism shields these issues from examination by constraining thought, while seeming to leave it entirely free, and by excluding considerations such as human differences and the nature of man and the good. The result is that rational discussion of human life becomes impossible, and the liberal view, which claims to treat everyone and everything the same, must be adopted as a supposedly neutral default.[6]

In abstract terms, the ability to suppress obviously relevant considerations results from the social power of liberal institutions and from the technological way of thinking that is now thought to exhaust rationality. That way of thinking cannot make sense of the good except as a matter of preference satisfaction. Nor is it able to discuss people in accordance with its own principles, while maintaining respect for them as human beings. For that reason it must treat people either as objects of manipulation or as inscrutable mysteries who cannot be judged and whose purposes must be accepted as final within the limits of a system that treats others the same. The latter approach is evidently more humane, so it is the one that must be chosen.

At a more personal level, the refusal to discuss basic issues is backed by self-satisfaction and arrogance. Our ruling class and its hangers-on are convinced they are radically superior, morally and intellectually, to everyone who has ever lived.[7] They have extricated themselves from inveterate error and now see the obvious, so that any drug-addled rocker against racism is justified in looking down on the saints and sages of the past. People were bigots then, and the views of bigots do not count, so why pay attention to them?

Quantity and Quality

The views now dominant seem obvious to educated and well-placed people, but the reaction only confirms that relevant con-

---

6 For other ways in which liberalism suppresses discussion, see 'Suppression of Discussion,' pp. 84 ff. above.

7 As Barack Obama has said, "We are the ones we've been waiting for."

siderations are being suppressed in a way that confirms such people's dominance. It is extremely improbable that we have suddenly become better and smarter than our predecessors. In fact, what has happened is that we have lost the ability to understand functional social patterns other than markets and bureaucracies. The result is that the past appears irrational, our society is plagued by dysfunctions we cannot understand or deal with, and we treat our own blindness and stupidity as the triumph of virtue and enlightenment.

Under such circumstances, each of us needs to make his own survey of the situation and decide what and whom to believe. The obvious way to decide basic issues, when ultimate principles are in dispute, is to look at overall consequences. If people really know better today, their superior understanding should make itself felt throughout intellectual and practical life. The record is at best mixed in that regard. Modern natural science has made our quantitative knowledge much more extensive and exact than in the past. With regard to quality, though, intangibles like artistic achievement suggest severe regression. That is a serious problem for the modern outlook, since qualitative judgments are more basic than quantitative ones. Scientific judgments require a system of practices already in place to tell us how to form, relate, and interpret them. How do we classify what we observe? Does an explanation make sense? How do we apply it? Such questions are far more a matter of what and how things are than how many they are, which means that they are basically qualitative.

For that reason, the difficulty people have today dealing with qualitative issues counsels skepticism regarding their judgments in general. This is all the more so the case, since inclusiveness and the cult of expertise insist on replacing common sense with an artificial system of thought that excludes important aspects of reality. We are told that common sense and long-accepted views are misleading, so we should accept on faith what the experts tell us. But how can we possibly trust people and ways of thinking that forbid us to think with our own minds and speak with our own voices?

Destructiveness

Some support for inclusiveness is well-intentioned. Nonetheless, as in the case of any movement that advantages some people at the expense of others, much of it is self-seeking. Support for inclusiveness is one way people identify with the ruling class and help it suppress its competitors, so that it has become a status marker. And affirmative action is in part an expression of dislike for ordinary white men, often on the part of whites who want to get a leg up at the expense of their fellows.

Stupidity and Corruption

Inclusiveness creates losers no less than exclusion does. Affirmative action is institutionalized injustice, with a direct victim for every direct beneficiary.[8] Frank Ricci, the lead plaintiff in the famous lawsuit over a written fireman's test in New Haven, is one of the few victims who successfully fought back, and he had to take his case all the way to the Supreme Court.[9]

Nor is it just those displaced by the less qualified who lose. Institutionalized lying and favoritism hurt everyone, especially when driven to ideological extremes.[10] Who wants a bumbling fireman? Who wants to ride on an airplane flown by an affirmative action pilot?[11] And who can doubt that medical school admission preferences kill patients? We all do better in an intelligently run society, and inclusiveness makes it impossible to discuss human affairs realistically. It has made obvious and important features of social life unmentionable. The resulting damage can be seen in top law schools, where the average black student is in the bottom 8 percent of his class because so many more are admitted

---

8 Lynch, *Invisible Victims: White Males and the Crisis of Affirmative Action.*

9 Ricci v. DeStefano, 129 S. Ct. 2658 (2009).

10 For a representative account of the degree of preference shown black students, see Armor, "Affirmative Action at Three Universities." For consequences of preferences in legal education, see Sander, "A Systemic Analysis of Affirmative Action in American Law Schools."

11 See Williams, "Gender-Norming Update," on mortal dangers posed by female affirmative-action Navy pilots.

than normal academic standards would justify.[12] The consequences can also be seen in the degradation of civil service tests resulting from fear of favoring whites,[13] the reckless mortgage lending promoted by refusal to look at the actual creditworthiness of minority borrowers,[14] and Nidal Malik Hasan, the affirmative-action military psychologist who murdered thirteen of his fellow soldiers as a consequence of Sudden Jihad Syndrome.[15]

Legitimation of Hatred

Antidiscrimination laws interfere arbitrarily in normal social functioning and create entitlements based on a few characteristics, principally race. The result is to destroy normal patterns of cooperation and set people against each other. Those disadvantaged by the system resent it, while beneficiaries justify it by keeping real or imagined grievances alive.

Resentment has its uses. Supporters of antidiscrimination laws exacerbate it though divisive rhetoric, propagation of horror stories, and violation of other laws in protest. Those at the top step in to maintain social peace in the face of the resulting ill-feeling by bribing the unruly at the expense of the productive and law-abiding. Claims of majority bigotry justify them in freeing themselves from popular control, since it is the bigoted middle that is blamed for social problems, and their hangers-on take advantage of the license such claims offer to abuse and cow their fellow citizens. Words like "racist" serve the same function "traitor" and "nigger" once did. They simplify political life by excluding from consideration the views and interests of those targeted. That is why President Bush called opposition to the Iraq war racist,[16]

---

12 More than 17 times as many. Thernstrom, "The Scandal of the Law Schools."

13 Sailer, "Test Case."

14 Sailer, "The Diversity Recession."

15 Spencer, "Army Ignored Warning Signs from Fort Hood Jihadist Because It 'Valued the Diversity of Having a Muslim Psychiatrist.'"

16. As the president said in a 2004 press conference,

There's a lot of people in the world who don't believe that people whose skin color may not be the same as ours can be free and self-govern. I reject that. I reject that and President Obama's supporters say the same about all opposition to the administration or its policies.

Such accusations are not purely cynical. Popular opposition to the established order is likely to be based on attitudes and understandings found more among some groups than others, so that bringing them into politics can be seen as an attempt by one group to dominate the others. If limited-government constitutionalism is mostly found among whites, and blacks and Hispanics mostly like active government, then limited-government constitutionalism must be racist. Also, the abolition of culture gives prominence to the crudest and most antisocial impulses, and, in the absence of social ties and an attractive conception of the good life, the basis for social cohesion can only be negative. The cohesion of the advanced liberal state therefore depends on hatred of its presumed enemies: racists, sexists, bigots, and homophobes. The concrete offenses may be fictional, but the hatred serves a necessary function, and the need for targets ensures a steady supply of well-publicized evildoers.[17]

Beneficiaries Injured

When we look at the situation candidly, it seems doubtful that many people gain overall from inclusiveness. Even supposed beneficiaries suffer, and not only from general social inefficiency. The civil rights revolution has led unsuccessful minorities to put their hopes in society in general, that is to say, the government, rather than each other and their own efforts, institutions, and relationships. The result is to suppress individual efforts and deprive troubled communities of a reality check.[18] It has also induced mainstream organizations to bribe talented minority group members away from their fellows, degrading community functioning and turning minority leadership into a privileged, self-seeking clique

---

strongly. I believe that people who practice the Muslim faith can self-govern. I believe that people whose skins aren't necessarily—are a different color than white can self-govern. —Will, "Time for Bush to See the Realities of Iraq."

17 The choice of villains is often ludicrously ill-advised, as in the Duke lacrosse and Trayvon Martin cases. On issues related to inclusiveness, good sense is evidently impossible for liberals.

18 Weissberg, "The Siren Song of Diversity."

that uses minority problems to extract additional benefits from white institutions for themselves and their supporters.

Inclusiveness degrades community functioning in other more fundamental ways as well. It insists on making traditional moral standards strictly private and so deprives them of authority, because the alternative would be cultural and lifestyle discrimination. The results include disruption of social functioning and liberation of destructive and self-destructive behavior. The weak and marginal become weaker and more marginal, resulting in special injury for those without resources and dependent on reliable connections to others. The post-1960s moral order, of which inclusiveness is a natural expression, has turned millions of people into criminals, drug addicts, crime victims, divorced and unwed mothers, abused and neglected children, homosexuals dead of AIDS, boys without fathers, and girls abused by their mothers' boyfriends. Should such people, those still alive,[19] at any rate, be grateful for it?

Inclusiveness also makes it risky to deal with those it intends to protect. Apparent qualifications become unreliable, and firing becomes difficult, if the situation does not work out. As a purely rational matter, it is better to have nothing to do with the protected or alternatively to play it safe, if indeed you cannot avoid dealing with them. The result is an increase in inequality within protected groups. Antidiscrimination laws help those whose membership in such groups seems accidental, since they appear safer to deal with, but hurt those intended to be helped most. Only a third of the black students admitted to Harvard are the American blacks intended to be benefited by affirmative action. The rest share the African, West Indian, or biracial origins of Barack Obama, Colin Powell, and Eric Holder.[20]

Affirmative action does not even satisfy those who have benefited most from it, since it induces them to build their careers on grievance and spend their lives working with people who they

19 See Tavernise, "Life Expectancy for Less Educated Whites in U.S. Is Shrinking"; Jonathan Tilove, "The Gap."

20 Rimer and Arenson, "Top Colleges Take More Blacks, but Which Ones?"

suspect would rather have nothing to do with them.[21] What does it do to people to live in such a way?[22] Can it be satisfying to live swaddled in patronizing lies that validate the prejudices they are intended to counteract? Is it helpful to put people in positions in which they are unable to perform up to standard? Surely people are able to sort out their connections better than government can. If there were no antidiscrimination laws, people who want to work together would find each other. In the long run, that would bring a better way of life and more happiness than current arrangements.

Specific Groups

Every group has a somewhat different situation, so it is worthwhile considering several of them at least briefly.

Blacks

Antidiscrimination laws and related developments are thought especially necessary for black people, but to all appearances they have mostly injured them. Barack Obama, Colin Powell, Condoleeza Rice, and Oprah do not refute the general tale of unsuccess.

The great initial push of the civil rights movement was for integrated schools. The effort succeeded in changing the law, but failed to achieve its goals with regard to either integration or educational progress. Blacks and whites still attend separate schools for the most part, and there are still huge gaps in achievement. The former situation does not seem to cause the latter, since the gaps remain even where schools are integrated,[23] and the success of historically black colleges suggests very strongly that black students do better in the basically separate environment that the law

---

21 For details, see Cose, *The Rage of a Privileged Class: Why Are Middle-Class Blacks Angry? Why Should America Care?*

22 Consider, for example, the account of the black professor of literature, Houston Baker, in Johnson, "Baker: In His Own Words."

23 Nor does the problem seem to be a lack of resources devoted to black education. See, e.g., Ciotti, *Money And School Performance: Lessons from the Kansas City Desegregation Experiment.*

views with abhorrence.[24] In any event, actual talent, learning, and effort matter more in the end than forced certification, so affirmative action does not benefit those it pushes into settings in which they are intellectually outclassed. Affirmative action in law school admissions, for example, means that blacks who go to law school generally struggle to pass the bar, and a majority never become lawyers at all.[25]

The next push was for jobs, but it is doubtful that antidiscrimination laws and related social changes have helped blacks overall from that standpoint either. Longstanding black economic progress accelerated after the Civil Rights Act of 1964, but then came to an end by 1975.[26] It appears that at least some of the stagnation can be attributed to the destruction of the basis for continued progress by the civil rights revolution and associated developments. If blacks live in an extensive free-market society with easy travel and good communications and have ordinary

24 USCCR, *The Educational Effectiveness of Historically Black College and Universities*. Also see Dreher, "The Failures Of Integration."

25 Sander, "A Systemic Analysis of Affirmative Action in American Law Schools."

26 Heckman and Payner, "Determining the Impact of Federal Antidisrimination Policy on the Economic Status of Blacks: A Study of South Carolina," lays out the general situation:

> The basic facts of black economic progress are well known. Since 1940, black wages and occupational status have improved, approaching the higher levels that whites enjoy. Beginning in 1965, the rate of improvement in black relative wages and occupational status accelerated. However, since 1975, relative black economic status has not advanced and may have deteriorated slightly.—p. 143, quoted in Epstein, *Forbidden Grounds: The Case Against Employment Discrimination Laws*, p. 243.

Figures on the percentages of black and white families in poverty fill out the picture to some degree. In 1966, those percentages were 35.5 and 9.3. By 1974, they had fallen to 26.9 and 6.8, by 1993, they had risen to 31.3 and 9.4, and by 1999, they had fallen again to 21.9 and 7.3. Throughout these periods, black families have been three to four times as likely as white families to be in poverty. *Historical Statistics of the United States, Millennial Edition*, Table Be283–309. As to more recent developments, it seems worth noting that gaps in median household wealth between whites, blacks, and Hispanics have recently risen to record highs. Kochhar, Fry, and Taylor, *Wealth Gaps Rise to Record Highs Between Whites, Blacks, Hispanics*.

liberty in economic, cultural, and religious matters, most of what their lives are like will end up depending on their cultural condition, which will in turn depend on the state of black communities. Since the '60s, the condition of these communities has taken a sharp turn for the worse. Affirmative action has stripped them of leaders, while feminism, sexual liberation, and the welfare system have radicalized the battle of the sexes and made the men all but irrelevant to family life.[27]

The result of such tendencies has been radical disruption of family, community, and personal life. Between 1970 and 2008, for example, the percentage of black children born to unmarried mothers went from 38 to 72 percent.[28] In 1960, 24.4 percent of black households were headed by women, in 1970, 34.5 percent, and, by 2000, 53.5 percent.[29] In 1960, 11.5 percent of the women who headed such households had never been married, by 2000 it was 64.8 percent.[30] The consequences for black men can be seen in prison populations.[31] In 1970, 35.8 percent of all prison inmates were black. In 2000, it was 46.3 percent of a much larger number.[32] The result, as of the beginning of this century, was that, on any given day, 30 percent of black men ages 20 to 29 were imprisoned or on probation or parole. A statistical model used by the

27 An additional problem is that a great many black men are dead or in otherwise missing. There are nearly 2 million more black women than men in America, and nearly a million black men in prison or the military, so in 2002 the total imbalance between the sexes was 2.8 million, or 26 percent. The comparable disparity for whites was 8 percent. Jonathan Tilove, "The Gap."

28 *Health, United States 2011: With Special Feature on Socioeconomic Status and Health*, 83, table 7.

29 Hacker, *Two Nations: Black and White, Separate, Hostile, Unequal*, 89.

30 Ibid., 96.

31 The consequences for men can also be seen in figures regarding relative earnings. In 1940, earnings of black male workers were 45 percent and black females 38 percent of those of whites. By 1960 the ratio had increased to 67 percent for men and 70 percent for women. In 1980, the figures were 75 percent and 92 percent and, in 2000, 74 percent and 94 percent. Progress did not stop after the Civil Rights Revolution, but it had become slower, especially for the men. Ibid., 119.

32 Ibid., 224. The figures cannot be explained by reference to racism in the criminal justice system. Mac Donald, "Is the Criminal-Justice System Racist?"

Bureau of Justice Statistics predicts that a young black man age 16 in 1996 faced a 29 percent chance of spending time in prison at some point during his life. The corresponding statistic for white men was 4 percent.[33] Given such figures, how can we view the post-1964 period as anything but catastrophic for black people?

The important question, of course, is how to go forward. It can hardly be helpful to view blacks as perpetual victims with no power over their own situation, especially if (as some say) stereotypes induce their own confirmation. As things stand, social obligations with regard to blacks are considered entirely open-ended. As long as blacks have problems, the problems are deemed to be the responsibility of society at large. Specific causality is irrelevant. Recent black arrivals and their descendants, like the President, the Attorney General, and Colin Powell, take advantage of affirmative action without feeling the need to express gratitude to those who provided them with something so valuable and so unmerited. Indeed, they take the view that too little is being done for them.

Justice O'Connor claimed in *Grutter*[34] that it will be possible to end affirmative action in 25 years. Promoters of reparations are bolder. They say the whole mess can be brought to an end by a one-shot payment. A century and a half after the end of black slavery in America, and half a century after *Brown v. Board* (1954) and the Civil Rights Act of 1964, who believes it? The system seems likely to perpetuate itself forever. Surely there is a better way.

Hispanics

Loss of legitimate particularity hurts Hispanics and other immigrants as well. Social scientists have long been puzzled by the "healthy immigrant paradox," the fact that new immigrants are healthier than second and third generation U.S. residents from the same countries. As one journalist notes, "various research has found that less-Americanized Hispanic children have healthier

---

33 Street, "Race, Prison, and Poverty: The Race to Incarcerate in the Age of Correctional Keynesianism."

34 Grutter v. Bollinger, 539 U.S. 306 (2003).

diets, better immunization rates, fewer suicide attempts, and decreased use of tobacco, alcohol and drugs than more Americanized adolescents."[35]

The paradox of declining well-being in the land of wealth and opportunity applies to behavioral matters in general, Hispanic teenagers who usually speak English are twice as likely to be sexually active as those who usually speak Spanish,[36] and conduct disorder, defined as "persistent patterns of child or adolescent behavior involving aggression or other violations of age-appropriate norms that cause significant clinical impairment," increases dramatically across generations after Mexicans migrate to the United States.[37]

The puzzle dissipates, if the situation is viewed from a human rather than technocratic point of view. Well-being is profoundly affected by how people live, and thus by the system of habits, attitudes, and connections that constitutes culture. Culture is particular and depends on setting, so migration into an alien environment disrupts it and degrades its ability to function. This is especially true, when cultural standards and their enforcement are intertwined with local kinship networks, as is the case with Mexican culture. The degradation increases, as assimilation goes forward, and, the more inclusive the society, the greater the disruption of informal networks and consequent degradation.

Immigration enthusiasts insist that assimilation works, since the children of Chinese immigrants quickly pick up American pop culture and learn how to get into top colleges. This is believable, but who wants the basis of our common life to be careerism and the habits and attitudes unsupervised teenagers pick up from uncultured peer groups operating in a commercialized and

---

35 Berger, "English Linked to Promiscuity in Hispanic Teens."

36 The numbers are quite striking. Among Hispanic teenagers in Arizona, 13.6 percent of Spanish speakers, 24.4 percent of bilinguals, and 30.7 percent of English speakers have engaged in sexual intercourse. Ibid.

37 Breslau J, "Migration from Mexico to the United States and Conduct Disorder." More generally, see Telles and Ortiz, *Generations of Exclusion: Mexican Americans, Assimilation, and Race*, which documents the failure of Mexican immigrants to assimilate and thrive.

burcaucracy-ridden environment? The more diverse our society, the less avoidable such a result becomes, and inclusiveness only guarantees that the problems will apply not only to immigrants, but to long-established native populations.

Women

It is quite natural that the sexual and feminist revolutions have made women unhappy.[38] Feminism separates women from the family, and so from a social institution that gives them an absolutely central place in the world they inhabit. It also weakens the family as such. Looser sex roles and sexual standards mean less mutual responsibility between the sexes and suppression of the masculine ideal, including concepts of protection and honor. The natural results are men women cannot rely on,[39] children without fathers, and feminized poverty.

Why should women want that? What they mostly want is marriage that works, support when they are bearing and raising children, and a favorable environment for those children to grow into.[40] They have been deprived of these things, but are supposedly compensated for the loss by the right to support themselves and their children by accepting subordinate positions in commercial organizations that view them as disposable profit centers. To

---

38 For the declining happiness of women in the feminist age, presented as a great paradox, see Stevenson and Wolfers, "The Paradox of Declining Female Happiness." Also see Angeles, "Children and Life Satisfaction," which reports that for married people, and especially for married women, children increase life satisfaction, and life satisfaction increases with the number of children. Previous researchers, who had ignored marriage as a variable (as they often do, in line with their technocratic preconceptions), had reported that children did not make people happy.

39 As Anthony Esolen notes, women do not civilize men, they domesticate them. It is the masculine timocracies that feminism targets which civilize men and make them useful as men. Esolen, "A College, of All Things."

40 In spite of claims to the contrary, marriage is indeed favorable to women's happiness and well-being. Yap, Anusic, and Lucas, "Does Personality Moderate Reaction and Adaptation to Major Life Events?"; Waite and Gallagher, *The Case for Marriage: Why Married People Are Happier, Healthier, and Better Off Financially*; Deparle, "Two Classes in America, Divided by 'I Do'."

help them do so, progressives give them the right to abortion and free contraception, the right to have other people raise their children for them, and the welfare state to fall back on, when additional help is needed. Why is the resulting situation better and more dignified than a position as wife, mother, and homemaker?

Sexual Minorities

Sexual liberation has meant glamorizing vice and destroying trust, loyalty, and complementarity in intimate relations. It has been a disaster for men, women, and children.[41] Nor has it benefited those whose impulses it has liberated most completely. Gay liberation has meant ever more radically disordered lives, epidemics of AIDS and other diseases, easier recruitment of vulnerable young people,[42] and the death of millions. The official expectation is that general social acceptance will give homosexual inclinations space to manifest their presumed goodness, when freely acted upon. There is no reason to believe it will have any such effect.[43] To all appearances, it is more likely to make homosexual behavior more widespread, extreme, and destructive.

Under such circumstances, why consider sexual and homosexual liberation a great step forward for anyone? Apart from its effect on those tempted to disordered conduct, it is at odds with any definite system of habits and expectations that orders the relations between men and women and gives those relations special status, function, and meaning. "Gay marriage," when taken seriously, destroys the possibility of understanding marriage as a natural institution that precedes the state and must be respected,

---

41 For a general discussion, see Eberstadt, *Adam and Eve After the Pill: Paradoxes of the Sexual Revolution.*

42 Baldwin, "Child Molestation and the Homosexual Movement"; Reisman, "Crafting Bi/Homosexual Youth."

43 See statistics cited in Cameron, *The Psychology of Homosexuality*; Cameron, *Medical Consequences of What Homosexuals Do*; Gallagher, "Don't Blame Me for Gay Teen Suicides." Also see Jones, "Sexual Orientation and Reason: On the Implications of False Beliefs About Homosexuality," on the untrustworthiness of official statements regarding homosexuality.

because it is uniquely suited to carry out fundamental social functions. For all these reasons, it makes no sense to consider the liberation of sexuality an advance for freedom. Instead, it is an aspect of the abolition of all modes of social functioning other than markets and bureaucracies. As such, it is part of the construction of the contemporary form of tyranny.

8

Liberalism and Its Competitors

Liberalism has not been the only principle for ordering society in the modern West. Until recently, it had to compete with other secular systems and accommodate traditional Christianity as well. Both competitors still have something of a presence. Their relation to liberalism is therefore worth discussion, both because the comparison helps bring out the specific qualities of liberalism and because liberalism will not last forever and one of its competitors may come back and replace it.

Alternative Modernities

Political modernity is a response to the abolition of the transcendent. Liberalism is the form that has won, and there are good reasons for its victory, but it not the only form of political modernity that has had some success. If life lacks a transcendent dimension, man might be viewed as fundamentally biological or historical or, in the alternative, as self-created. Moderns have correspondingly tried to base social order on biology, history, or the triumph of the will.

Biology

Scientism favors physical explanations, so that the most direct response to modernity is the attempt to base social order on the physical aspects of man's being. The usual physicalist view is that natural selection, or to put it in Darwin's terms, "the preservation of favoured races in the struggle for life," explains human nature and behavior. Thus, physicalists have often viewed racial struggle as fundamental.

A basic problem with that view is that what people find worthwhile in life cannot be reduced to the survival and multiplication of an extended kinship group. For this reason, the latter cannot serve as the guiding principle of social order.[1] This is why the extreme nationalists and racists of the last century ended up emphasizing arbitrary will more than biology and relying on theatrics, irrationalism, and violence to overcome the intellectual weakness of their position.

The same basic problem applies to any other merely biological understanding of human life, construing life, for example, as a matter of providing for man's physical needs and keeping his actions from leading to catastrophes such as nuclear war or radical environmental degradation. Such concerns are important, but they are not enough to live by, so they are not enough to motivate an overall system of politics.

History

Secular conservatives, who are moderates among modernists, have tried to mitigate the effect of their basic anti-transcendental commitments by basing social order on habit and history. They hold a basically modern view of reality, reason, and knowledge, but accept that we do not have an effective technology of social life. For this reason, they accept experience as their guide and, with it, the necessity of the inherited, informal, and pre-rational aspects of social order.

Such an approach has failed, even though their acceptance of modernist principles has enabled them to play a fairly prominent role in mainstream politics. As proponents of traditional ways and attachments, secular conservatives have favored particularity and the practices, conditions, and institutions that allow it to maintain itself and function. In present-day America, these include federalism, local autonomy, traditional marriage, immigration restrictions, limitations on the welfare state, and respect for the right of families and religious and community institutions to run their own affairs.

---

1 See Gottfried, "The Limits of Race."

They have continually given ground on all those issues. Their weakness has been especially apparent in connection with inclusiveness. Apart from illegal immigration and "affirmative action," which are sore points for voters, conservative politicians have been willing to swear devotion to an anti-discrimination regime that is at odds with any possible conservatism. Even opposition to affirmative action and illegal immigration has been lukewarm and sporadic, more a matter of opportunistic gestures than a principled effort to change law and policy.

The failure was preordained, since how the world is understood shapes political commitments. Secular conservatives do not seriously dispute fundamental current understandings, and such understandings make serious opposition to liberalism seem irrational and wrong. Why expect those who accept them to mount a successful resistance? As moderns, secular conservatives accept satisfaction of preferences as the rational guide to action. As conservatives, they need people to act on other principles, but offer them no persuasive reason to do so, when it becomes inconvenient.[2] Continuity and respect for traditional ways may be a good thing in general, but there are exceptions, and why should my case not be an exception?

Triumph of the Will

Abolishing transcendence abolishes the distinction between preference satisfaction and the good, so that satisfaction of preferences becomes the rational purpose of all action. The most rational political response to modernity is therefore the attempt to derive moral and social order from maximum preference satisfaction.

Preferences conflict, however, and whose should prevail when

---

2 As Roger Scruton puts it,

Burke brought home to me that our most necessary beliefs may be both unjustified and unjustifiable from our own perspective, and that the attempt to justify them will lead merely to their loss. . . . The real justification for a prejudice is the one which justifies it as a prejudice, rather than as a rational conclusion of an argument. In other words it is a justification that cannot be conducted from our own perspective, but only from outside, as it were, as an anthropologist might justify the customs and rituals of an alien tribe.—Scruton, "Why I Became a Conservative."

they oppose each other? The obvious answer is to prefer one's own, but "looking out for number one" is not, at least without severe limitation, a principle of social order. Since man is social, it does not even work in private life.

FASCISM AND BOLSHEVISM

It is not easy to make arbitrary will a principle of public order. Anti-liberal moderns resolve the paradox by appealing to collective power. The will of the individual is absorbed in that of the people, party, or state, and this will, embodied in the will of the supreme leader, overcomes all others and establishes order. The motive for participation in the effort, and thus the basis for loyalty to the regime, becomes the joy of smashing the opposition, together with comradeship in the struggle to make the willed order prevail.

A problem with the solution is that anti-liberal moderns are moderns. As such, it is natural for them to view collectivities as arbitrary constructions. What is special about the proletariat or the German people? Whom do they include and why? Why are Stalin and Hitler their perfect representatives? And why are my will and theirs the same? Such questions are unanswerable, and fascists and communists thus embraced irrationalism and relied quite directly on lies and violence as the basis for their rule.

The result was catastrophic. The anti-liberal modernists took as their principle of social order what some of them called "life," the expression of the power of the order itself. In the absence of substantive goods, this principle could manifest itself only through self-assertion against opposition, the more extreme the better. Infinite victory in infinite war became the ruling ideal of social life. A society that places itself on such a basis is not going to last. It will overreach and destroy itself, like the Nazis, or sink into posturing, hypocrisy, and corruption that eventually becomes terminal, like the Soviets after Stalin.

LIBERALISM

Liberalism defers and defuses the problem posed by the sovereignty of human will by claiming that it progressively maximizes the equal satisfaction of all preferences. The will is to be tamed by the equal sovereignty of other wills and the demands of a technically rational system. Arbitrary power and social conflict vanish.

The peacefulness of this ideal has enabled liberalism to outlast communism, fascism, and Nazism. Nonetheless, those forms of modernity responded to a real problem. By abolishing all goods that transcend individual preferences, the modern outlook radically separates individual from social goals. There is no rational way to re-integrate them within the limits of modernity, so an ideological myth is needed. Fascists and communists deal with the problem in a straightforward way by making the People, Party, or State absolute and reducing the individual to part of the collectivity. If this absolute is accepted—and those who reject it soon disappear from the discussion—integration of individual and collectivity is a matter of course.

The liberal myth is more subtle. Instead of absorbing the individual into the collectivity, it reduces the collectivity to the individual. It presents the liberal state as government by and for the people, here to serve them and acting only to promote their freedom and equality. What that state imposes is reduced without remainder to individual desire and content-free public rationality. Obedience to it is not subservience, but only intelligent promotion of what each of us already wants.

Such is the official story. In fact, of course, liberal government is like other government. It is run not by the many, but by the few, and is less democratic and individualistic than technological and manipulative. Those who rule try to make their life easier by accommodating popular concerns, but their guiding principle is less the will of the people than staying in power and running things in accordance with their own interests and understandings, which mostly have to do with turning the society into an efficient machine with themselves at the top.

Nor can liberal government really favor equal freedom, since some must lose in the event of conflict. In any event, we often choose things other than satisfaction of desire: God, country, and family; the good, beautiful, and true; adventure, struggle, and comradeship. To the extent we prefer such things to getting our own way simply as such, liberalism makes no sense. It "gives us what we want," but we reject this as unworthy, so it is not what we want.

To avoid such problems, liberal government has to tell us what to want. It allows us a safe and moderate desire for what suits the regime: career, consumption, and various private indulgences. Everything else it denounces as oppressive and forbids as disruptive. Liberalism thus forbids us to want the things people care about most deeply. The authorities from which it frees us—religion, family, particular culture and people—are those that enable us to act independently of formal institutions controlled by those at the top. It therefore gives us the freedom of dependency on a featureless structure that cares nothing for us and rejects our fundamental concerns. Why is this something to which we should aspire?

Christianity

Pre-modern Western society was based on Christianity, local traditions, and general understandings of what is natural and good. Modernity attacks all these things, and some Christians have proposed sidestepping the attack and making peace with modernity by divorcing their faith from other pre-modern principles. This proposal usually takes the form of abandoning tradition and natural law in favor of liberal Christianity or Christian liberalism, and it has become a source of fundamental contention among Christians. Some say that Christianity must change or die, and express itself by reference to contemporary understandings and concerns. Others say that it can only live through what it has received and that, if it makes contemporary views the standard, it will substitute another revelation for the Christian one.

Inclusivist Christianity

Liberalism has the support of all respected social authorities today. It should surprise no one that religious leaders have lined themselves up on the side of the rest of the credentialed, verbal, and managerial classes by adopting it. In the age of prince-bishops, ecclesiastics had a soft spot for princes. Times have changed, and political temptations with them. The result is that mainstream Christian leaders today try to be as liberal as possible, bending or abandoning awkward doctrines to the extent their ecclesial communities allow them to do so. They present Christianity as largely a spiritualized form of liberalism and have come to see exclusion in the current liberal sense as liberals see it, so that its eradication seems to them a fundamental moral and social imperative.

Such tendencies are nonetheless odd, given fundamental Christian loyalties. Inclusiveness is not Christianity. It has nothing to do with the love of God, and its rejection of natural law means it has no distinct conception of the good of man. In any event, it is impossible to disconnect Christianity from tradition and natural law. Tradition is necessary to a system that sees man as oriented toward goods he does not fully grasp, natural law to a religion that believes that God created the world, found it good, and was able to manifest Himself through it. If the world does not embody intrinsic meanings, purposes, and goods, how can God express himself so fully within it as to become incarnate? And to make matters worse, inclusiveness is an intolerant outlook that feels called upon to use compulsion to remake all human relationships in its image. As such, it is an existential enemy of Christianity because it can allow Christianity no space of its own to operate.

The Catholic View

Since church spokesmen have occupational biases that sometimes lead them to present their faith badly, it seems reasonable to look at the issues in the light of the basic principles and authorities they accept as binding. This will be easiest and perhaps most useful in the case of Roman Catholicism, the largest Christian communion and the one with the best-defined body of doctrine.

WHERE CAN IT BE FOUND?

But what is the Catholic view and where do we find it? The phrase can mean anything from the view that best fits the basic Catholic understanding of the world to the predominant view of average Catholics at a particular time and place. As a day-to-day matter, people mostly take it to be the view expressed by Catholic functionaries. If the United States Conference of Catholic Bishops puts out a statement, that is the Catholic position.[3]

Such statements need careful reading, however, because the way bishops and other Church spokesmen talk about political and social issues has changed over the years. As the Church modernized and bureaucratized after Vatican II, pronouncements by bishops and their growing professional staffs have tended to draw less on Church tradition and more on the outlook of secular functionaries.[4] This trend has been encouraged by the tendency in the post-Vatican II Church to try to engage the world by emphasizing points of agreement and using the language of the world, which in a liberal setting means using expressions like "rights"[5] and "discrimination," to express its own thoughts.

Such developments have made Church pronouncements more pleasing to *The New York Times*, but perhaps less clearly reflective of Catholic thought as a whole. Even when the substance of a pronouncement is at odds with anything the *Times* might say, as it generally is, the differences often seem less important than they should. The result of such trends is that day-to-day statements by Church officials on discrimination and related issues often seem more consistent with the advanced liberal view than they are or should be.[6]

But if bishops and bishops' conferences cannot always be relied on for a clear statement of Catholic teaching, and even informal papal pronouncements can be misleading, where do you look? It is an awkward question for a layman, since the hierarchy are authorized interpreters of Catholic belief, and laymen are not. Life poses awkward questions, however, and, in any event, Catholicism does not claim to make thought unnecessary, but to

3 The Church herself does not normally give such statements teaching authority. Pope John Paul II, "Apostolos Suos."

4 Conner, "Social Teachings At Risk In The American Catholic Church."

5 See Feser, "Stupak's Enablers?", for a discussion of "rights" in a Catholic context.

6 See, e.g., Pope Benedict XVI, "Angelus"; Pope John Paul II, "Message of the Holy Father John Paul II for the 89th World Day of Migrants and Refugees"; Catholic Bishops' Conference of England & Wales, *Diversity and Equality Guidelines*.

make it productive by illuminating the principles governing man and the world.

Catholics believe simply as Catholics that authoritative Church statements, that is to say, statements from popes and general councils that are intended to establish a particular teaching, are reliable. Since the Church is very careful when she makes such statements, they should be of interest to non-Catholics as well. Intelligent, responsible, and experienced men who care about the long-term effects of what they say have thought them through.

At this high level, there are not many clear general statements about discrimination and related topics. This is not surprising, since most statements about those topics by anyone anywhere are indefinite, specialized, contradictory, tendentious, or mindlessly dogmatic. Human distinctions and their social settings and functions are infinitely varied, so worthwhile categorical statements are hard to come by, and the ones available are often tendentious and of low intellectual quality. It is to the Church's credit that she has said so little that is intended to be authoritative on the subject.

WHAT IS IT?

In general, though, the view evident in authoritative Church statements is that race, culture, religion, sex, and so on do not determine human worth and have often been applied abusively, but are nonetheless legitimate human distinctions that can legitimately affect how we treat people. Such a view lends no support to the advanced liberal view or the current antidiscrimination regime.

The most basic statements, of course, are found in the Bible, and here the part people refer to is Paul's statement in Galatians 3:28:

> There is neither Jew nor Greek: there is neither bond nor free: there is neither male nor female. For you are all one in Christ Jesus.

People often treat those words as if they were a manifesto for contemporary left-wing egalitarianism. They are not. Paul is emphasizing the unity of Christians as forcefully as possible by saying it trumps the most basic human distinctions, so he cannot possibly be saying that there is something specially bad about distinctions relating to race, class, and gender compared with other distinctions. To the contrary, he is implying that they are the ones that are most enduringly important. If they were not, he would have mentioned the other more important distinctions instead.

He is saying, of course, that the trio do not affect ultimate human worth, but the same is true *a fortiori* of other less basic distinctions. One could also say that in Christ Jesus there is neither professor nor janitor, neither Supreme Court justice nor used car salesman. That would not mean that these distinctions are illegitimate, only that they are not ultimate for a God "who maketh his sun to rise upon the good, and bad, and raineth upon the just and the unjust."[7] So the verse lends no support to the view that there is something specially toxic about different treatment based on distinctions like sex and ancestry.

On that point, Paul's well-known comments on the role of women, and 1 Timothy 5:8, which deals with the practical aspects of day-to-day life, are more relevant:

> But if any man have not care of his own, and especially of those of his house, he hath denied the faith, and is worse than an infidel.

Particular distinctions and connections matter, and charity begins at home. What could be more at odds with today's concept of inclusiveness?

Moving forward 1900 years, the most comprehensive, authoritative, and relevant non-scriptural statement relating to equality and discrimination is probably section 29 of *Gaudium et Spes*, one of the documents of the Second Vatican Council:

> The basic equality of all must receive increasingly greater recognition. . . . With respect to the fundamental rights of the person, every type of discrimination, whether social or cultural, whether based on sex, race, color, social condition, language or religion, is to be overcome and eradicated as

---

7 Matthew 5:45.

contrary to God's intent. . . . Therefore, although rightful differences exist between men, the equal dignity of persons demands that a more humane and just condition of life be brought about. For excessive economic and social differences between the members of the one human family or population groups cause scandal, and militate against social justice, equity, the dignity of the human person, as well as social and international peace.[8]

It seems, then, that, with respect to fundamental rights, the Church opposes discrimination based on sex, race, and indeed anything whatever. It also favors basic equality and opposes excessive inequalities, while recognizing rightful differences.

People often talk as if these principles support antidiscrimination and inclusiveness as currently understood. They obviously do not. Not all inequalities are excessive, and, if something is our fundamental right as persons, then we have it just by being persons, regardless of what else we might be. We have it, if we are men or women and also if we are illiterate pickpockets, Tahitian bodybuilders, Catholic archbishops, or anything else. In each of these cases, we have the equal right not to be robbed or murdered, to a fair trial if someone is going to put us in prison, and to many other things. We obviously do not have to be treated the same in all respects. There exist, as the Council Fathers note, rightful differences. A Catholic archbishop does not as such have exactly the same position, in the Church or secular society, as an illiterate pickpocket or Tahitian bodybuilder (assuming, of course, that they are all different persons).

To all appearances, then, race, culture, sex, religion, and the like remain for the Church legitimate human distinctions that can have legitimate effects, just as other human distinctions can. The point comes out most clearly with regard to the position of women. Women cannot be discriminated against with regard to fundamental rights, and

---

8 Second Vatican Council, "Pastoral Constitution on the Church in the Modern World."

access to employment and to professions must be open to all without unjust discrimination: men and women, healthy and disabled, natives and immigrants.[9]

Nonetheless, women cannot be priests. This is not an unjust discrimination. Nor is the restriction of the ordained priesthood to men some strange arbitrary divine command that is at odds with everything else that is right and good in human relations. As Bl. John Paul II notes, "women occupy a place, in thought and action, which is unique and decisive."[10] In other words, "equality" and "nondiscrimination" do not mean there is no difference in the social position and function of the sexes. Indeed, the Church says the contrary:

> The Church can and should help modern society by tirelessly insisting that the work of women in the home be recognized and respected by all in its irreplaceable value.... Possible discrimination between the different types of work and professions is eliminated at its very root once it is clear that all people, in every area, are working with equal rights and equal responsibilities.... Society must be structured in such a way that wives and mothers are not in practice compelled to work outside the home, and that their families can live and prosper in a dignified way even when they themselves devote their full time to their own family.... Furthermore, the mentality which honors women more for their work outside the home than for their work within the family must be overcome.[11]

So the unjust discrimination the Church opposes is quite different from the discrimination the Civil Rights Act of 1964 forbids. What she means by "unjust discrimination" is not difference in treatment as such, but abusive difference in treatment that does not serve the common good and respect those subject to it. Promoting recognition of a distinction in function between the

---

9 Catholic Church, *Catechism of the Catholic Church.*
10 Pope John Paul II, "Evangelium Vitae."
11 Pope John Paul II, "Apostolic Exhortation Familiaris Consortio."

sexes is not that kind of discrimination and, in fact, is a good idea that we should all favor. Indeed, it is radical sexual egalitarianism that is unjustly discriminatory, since it discriminates against the work in the home that women have traditionally performed and for which they have a special gift.

The Church, then, does not support anything like what is generally called feminism. From an actual feminist point of view, she is incurably sexist. And, from a Catholic point of view, actual feminism is wrong. That is why in *Evangelium Vitae* Bl. John Paul II called for a "new feminism" that would respect the "true genius of women." Liberals consider such statements evidence of the incoherence of an official Catholic position that both favors and opposes "discrimination." What they show instead is that the Church does not agree with liberals on equality issues, even though she tends at present (wisely or unwisely) to use similar words.

The evidence as to discrimination related to ethnicity and culture is less specific, but the same principles evidently apply. The Church says it is against "racism," which has an extremely broad meaning in public discussion today. Nonetheless, Christianity is not Islam, which merges the nations into a single *Ummah,* conforming to a single law. Perhaps for this reason, the Bible accepts the existence of different peoples as normal and legitimate.[12] It is acceptable, from a Catholic perspective, for Jews and Poles, and Israel and Poland, to exist and function, each in a distinctive way, even though their separate existence and functioning require distinctions, boundaries, line-drawing, and exclusions relating to ethnicity, and even though ethnic loyalty and nationalism sometimes lead to abuses.

More generally, Pope Pius XII noted that

There exists an order established by God, which requires a more intense love and a preferential good done to those people that are joined to us by special ties. Even our Lord

---

12 See Berthoud, "The Bible and the Nations, Part 1"; Berthoud, "The Bible and the Nations, Part 2"; Berthoud, "The Bible and the Nations, Part 3."

has given the example of this preference towards the country, when He cries on the destruction of Jerusalem.[13]

That view is solidly supported by Saint Thomas, who notes that, after duties toward God, we owe most to those to whom we are most closely connected, beginning with parents and other blood relatives:[14]

Man is debtor chiefly to his parents and his country, after God. Wherefore just as it belongs to religion to give worship to God, so does it belong to piety, in the second place, to give worship to one's parents and one's country.

The worship due to our parents includes the worship given to all our kindred, since our kinsfolk are those who descend from the same parents. . . . The worship given to our country includes homage to all our fellow-citizens and to all the friends of our country.[15]

The Church thus recognizes that blood ties, including extended blood ties and communal ties generally, are entirely legitimate. It is right to have a preferential option for your own people.

Some degree of discrimination based on ties like blood and culture is thus normal and good. This point is strengthened by the very high value placed on particular community and culture. As Pius XI noted,

The Church's maternal heart is big enough to see in the God-appointed development of individual characteristics and gifts, more than a mere danger of divergency. She rejoices at the spiritual superiorities among . . . nations.[16]

And Bl. John Paul II says:

13 Cited in Williamson, "A Practicing Catholic Considers Why 'The Church' Is Wrong About Immigration."

14 See Aquinas, "Summa Theologica, Second Part of the Second Part, Question 26, Articles 6–8."

15 Aquinas, "Summa Theologica, Second Part of the Second Part, Question 101, Article 1."

16 Pope Pius XI, "Mit Brennender Sorge."

By receiving and inheriting faith and the values and elements that make up the culture of your society and the history of your nation, each one of you is spiritually endowed in your individual humanity. Here we come back to the parable of the talents, the talents which we receive from the Creator through our parents and families, and also through the national community to which we belong.[17]

Man is understood in a more complete way when he is situated within the sphere of culture through his language, history, and the position he takes towards the fundamental events of life, such as birth, love, work and death. At the heart of every culture lies the attitude man takes to the greatest mystery: the mystery of God. Different cultures are basically different ways of facing the question of the meaning of personal existence.[18]

If particular cultures and national communities have such importance for the way we become human and connect to God, then an understanding of diversity and inclusion that abolishes legitimate boundaries between them and so makes them nonfunctional cannot be acceptable, and multiculturalism, which deprives every culture of any setting of its own in which it can function as authoritative, must be wrong.

It is evident, then, that the Catholic view of ethnic and similar distinctions is not at all the same as the advanced liberal view. On the former view, actions helpful in maintaining the identity and functionality of national or ethnic cultures are in general right and indeed praiseworthy, as long as they do not involve contempt and abuse for other people. There is no reason this principle should apply to minority cultures, but not others, and it appears to apply quite generally. After all, in a globalized world, *every* culture and people is an endangered minority with an identity and specific way of life that is threatened by current trends. It is therefore relevant that Bl. John Paul II noted in *Dilecti Amici*, addressing the youth of the world:

17 Pope John Paul II, "Evangelium Vitae."
18 Pope John Paul II, "Centesimus Annus."

In regard to this inheritance [of faith, culture, and national history] we cannot maintain a passive attitude, still less a defeatist one. . . . We must do everything we can to accept this spiritual inheritance, to confirm it, maintain it and increase it. This is an important task for all societies, especially perhaps . . . for those that must defend from the danger of destruction from outside or of decay from within the very existence and essential identity of the particular nation.[19]

Such statements are obviously relevant to issues relating to immigration, diversity, and inclusion, and they do not favor the liberal position. It seems clear, then, that the implications of the Catholic view are not at all what they are commonly thought to be. Since it is the best-developed form of the Christian view and the one to which most Christians are at least formally committed, it should be persuasive to those who consider the Christian view of equality relevant at all.

Whom Would Jesus Exclude?

The relation between Christianity and social life is necessarily complex, and inclusivist Christianity is pop theology Christianity. Asking about Jesus and exclusion is like asking whom he would shoot, fire, lock up, expel from school, or turn down as a bad credit risk. He did not deal with such issues and had no occasion to do so. As man, he was unmarried, unemployed, without property, and homeless. As God, he was lord of all things. The distinctions "mine" and "thine," "ours" and "yours," which give rise to everyday exclusions, were not normally an issue for him in either role.[20]

Christians must nonetheless deal with them. For that reason they accept jails, armies, private property, and other institutions that involve inequality and coercion and are often, like all aspects of human life, intertwined with injustice. Nor is acceptance a

19 Pope John Paul II, "Apostolic Letter Dilecti Amici of Pope John Paul II to the Youth of the World on the Occasion of International Youth Year."

20 He did, however, distinguish those who accepted him from those who did not, a distinction that now makes mainstream Christians rather uncomfortable.

matter of accomplishment falling short of ideals. Man is social and relies on institutions, so that "love thy neighbor" includes support for basic social institutions and the disciplines and distinctions on which they depend. We render unto Caesar that which is Caesar's and, for the same reason, we render what is due to property, family, community, and cultural group and accept the boundaries and exclusions through which such things exist and function.[21]

Christians are able to do so in good conscience, because they do not view the resulting inequality and coercion, or the human flaws that can make them oppressive, as ultimate. Created things have inevitable limitations, and we live in a fallen world, but Christianity offers a way to transcend limitations and restore what is fallen through principles that place differences in perspective and make them part of a higher unity in which each contributes to the others, while maintaining its distinctiveness. It is radically at odds with liberal modernity, which abolishes the transcendent for the sake of a doomed attempt to construct a wholly this-worldly realm of peace, justice, and radical equality.

21 As the Catechism says, "Society ensures social justice when it provides the conditions that allow associations or individuals to obtain what is their due, according to their nature and their vocation." Catholic Church, *Catechism of the Catholic Church*, paragraph 1928.

9

Back to the Center

Freedom, equality, diversity, tolerance, and inclusiveness trump all other considerations today. They forbid us to tell others what to do, so that the world has to be run impersonally, that is, by experts, bureaucrats, and managers who claim their determinations are based on neutral grounds that have nothing to do with personal wishes. Traditional arrangements such as family and religion, which are not based on neutral procedures, must be treated as optional private pursuits and so deprived of any serious function. Representative institutions remain, and they seem to stand for a principle of non-expert rule, but their power is more and more restricted. They become a way of registering the public's approval of decisions arrived at in other ways.

Fundamental Flaws

To all appearances, no educated, sane, and well-intentioned person sees a problem with such arrangements. Let each do what he wants, subject to the equal right of others to do the same, and let those who know best decide public policy, subject to popular approval. What could be more reasonable and just? Nonetheless, perfect solutions rarely work as intended. Life is too complex for experts to master, the result being that, when they run the world, they end up deciding issues arbitrarily or avoiding them altogether. The result is incapacity disguised as perfect rationality, and that is what we see around us. Public life has reached a dead end. In economics, domestic policy, and international relations, problems mount up and no one knows what to do about them. On social issues, which include inclusiveness, we are stuck with dogmas like "diversity is strength" that make intelligent discussion impossible.

How can we be in such a fix, if our understandings are so advanced? In fact, it is our supposed expertise and enlightenment that make it impossible to understand and deal with the problems of social life. More and more, it seems that among us:

- Freedom means comprehensive control of human relations, so we do not oppress each other.

- Equality means rule by irresponsible and unrepresentative elites who keep us equal by keeping us powerless.

- Reason means submission of mind and will to the authority of experts.

- Diversity and inclusiveness mean distinctions cannot be allowed to matter, so they have to be neutered or destroyed.

- Tolerance means the demonization of those attached to nonliberal principles as bigots and fundamentalists.

- Giving people what they want means destroying the goods they care about most, since those goods cannot be produced and distributed to order.

Such contradictions reflect problems within liberalism and modernity that go down to the most basic issues, issues as basic as how we acquire knowledge and choose goals. Liberal modernity tries to deal with such issues in a clear, rational, and progressive way by simplifying them, so that the world can be understood, managed, and put right. With this in mind, it makes knowledge strictly public and goods strictly private. If you want to know what is true, you ask experts who determine the answer by objective critical standards. With respect to the good and beautiful, however, there is no knowledge, but only preference, which means that each of us defines his own goals and values. The alternative would be to allow people claiming special knowledge of the good to force their preferences on others, and that would be oppressive.

Such an approach seems the perfection of reason and tolerance to those brought up in it, but it has consequences that are very different in character. One problem is that insistence on the subjectivity of preference and objectivity of knowledge introduces a sort of division of labor that makes ordinary people incompetent to decide anything that matters. We are free to choose our goals, liberal modernity tells us, but we cannot know how to attain them, because we are not experts and lack knowledge. Further, our goals are individual and arbitrary, so they oppose others' goals. We cannot deal with the resulting conflicts by ourselves, since we simply want what we want and, even if willing to compromise, have no way to determine who should give way on what to whom. It follows that, for liberals, we cannot act on our own understanding in any matter that makes much difference to anyone. Experts have to arrange matters for our own good and that of others. Otherwise, we will injure ourselves or infringe on equal freedom and respect. Further, we must give up all goals that have a social character and do not directly support the system. Such goals are awkward to manage and are sure to conflict with the goals of other people. So our goals must be either politically correct or entirely private.

As time goes by, the experts responsible for determining the demands of equal freedom find more and more to supervise and become more and more intrusive. Thus, it turns out that, when freedom and equality are treated as ultimate standards, they lead to an ever-greater degree of subordination and constraint. The ultimate result is complete tutelage, with kindergarten as the model for social life.[1] However entrenched such a system may be at present, it is too contradictory to last.

Self-Destruction

As a highest principle, equal freedom ends in soft, smothering tyranny. Such a tyranny is likely to become increasingly chaotic. Systems tend toward entropy, political systems being like all others. This tendency is strengthened in the case of liberal inclusiveness by the liberal dislike of explicit coercion and by the destruction of

---

1 For an analysis of the situation from an energetic classical liberal perspective, see Furedi, *On Tolerance: A Defence of Moral Independence*. Also consider the popularity of Fulghum, *All I Really Need To Know I Learned in Kindergarten*.

informal and implicit principles of social order. Liberal principles aspire to universality, and so they suppress non-liberal traditions and practices that involve exclusion on grounds now forbidden. They are also progressive, valuing clarity and logic and insisting on continual self-purification. The result is that they destroy the conditions of their own functioning. They sacrifice social ties to self-definition and erode the standards of competence and the informal habits and understandings needed for formal public institutions to work. Such effects can be masked to some degree by the refusal to recognize them and by making them universal and thus part of the general conditions of life. Nonetheless, they are real and lead to increasingly radical dysfunction. The question is how much damage they will do while they are with us and what will happen when the system falls apart.

Where they cannot create, utopias destroy. When inclusiveness destroys the concreteness and specificity of culture, it destroys the possibility of a civilized and humane way of life. The recent history of Russia, featuring failed socialism followed by colossal thievery and mafia rule, shows what happens upon the collapse of a sustained and determined effort to eradicate a basic social principle founded on natural human tendencies. The principle comes back, but in a crude form cut loose from the connections that once limited and civilized it, and the result is the opposite of what was intended. Russian socialism ended in the reign of lawless greed, and Western multiculturalism will very likely end in a radically divided society shot through with hatred and violence.

The accepted view is that those who oppose liberalism, especially its inclusivist aspects, do so for bad motives. The view is unjust, but it may reflect a premonition of the future. Discrimination does not mean Nazism any more than the state means Fascism,[2] but moderns find it hard to maintain distinctions.

---

2 The state does have its troublesome aspects. Its rise and consolidation meant war and ethnic cleansing in early modern Europe, as it has recently in the Levant. In 1500 there were no Jews legally present in any European state on the Atlantic seaboard. Today there are fewer and fewer Jews or Christians in the lands (other than Israel) that were part of the Ottoman Empire in 1914.

Modernity tries to establish a unitary system that makes everything controllable and, to that end, breaks down complex networks of relationships in favor of simple distinctions, oppositions, and subordinations. The result is a tendency toward political extremism of one sort or another. It is therefore quite possible that the collapse of inclusiveness will lead to extremes of discrimination, just as the collapse of state socialism in Russia led to violent extremes of greed.

Nonetheless, the answer to the danger of extremism is not a contrary extremism, but understanding the principles at work and trying to balance and moderate them. All social authorities and institutions involve inequalities. We cannot escape danger by destroying what allows life to be complex and therefore human, and so a broad range of inequalities should be allowed. The risk of doing so is part of the risk of living, and the alternative is to make inequalities fewer, but more extreme.

A Return to Sanity

The risks of the present situation are serious and must be averted if at all possible. To do so, we must examine what has gone wrong and where we are headed, and then change course. This will involve dealing with the most basic principles governing life and thought. It will be difficult to do so. Basic issues are hard to grasp whole, while alternatives are hard to define and make concrete, and people find it difficult to understand what is at issue. In addition, modern ways of thinking have a viral genius for invading, colonizing, and destroying other traditions.[3] The result is that public discussion has fallen into a black hole from which our situation is all but invisible to educated people.

Nonetheless, we have no choice but to try. Ultimate standards matter, and, the greater the power of a destructive principle, the more important it is to understand and resist it. The present situation is the result of an intellectual revolution that has run into trouble because of its poverty of resources, and a failing revolu-

---

3 See Salingaros, "The Derrida Virus," for the specific case of deconstruction.

tion eventually falls apart and gives way to something quite different. The task of those who see the problem is to work, so that what replaces the present system is something better, our best hope being forthright analysis and criticism based on more reasonable understandings. Such an approach may point toward a more functional and beneficial system, or at least promote moderation and good sense, as events play out. In any event, clarification of thought is likely to help us toward a better life for ourselves and is worth pursuing for that reason alone.

Problems With Scientism

Scientism, which tells us that modern natural science is the whole of knowledge, is the view of knowledge and reality that now makes liberalism impregnable by excluding the discussion of goods and of natural patterns. It is a fallacious view, because it takes part of reason and treats it as the whole. Modern natural science is obviously incomplete as a system. It assumes certain principles that it does not prove or justify, for example, the relevance of the past to the future. Also, it depends on informal personal knowledge and the ability to recognize and deal with functional systems, that is, with formal and final cause. For example, it requires scientific researchers to be able to recognize their apparatus, know how it works, set it up to do what they want, tell whether it is working properly, operate it, read it, and interpret the readings. It also requires trust in the scientific community. Laymen and scientists must assume that a recognizable social network of human beings will routinely succeed in sorting through possible theories and picking out the ones that are best supported and therefore most likely to be true, at least in general, in the long run, and to an extent that makes scientific consensus reliable on the whole.

It may be reasonable for us to rely on scientists and for scientists to feel at home with their equipment and generally trust each other, and I believe it is, but doing so depends on insight, judgment, and faith. We must, for example, be able to recognize genuine scientists and serious work and distinguish them from frauds, and there is no scientific way to do so. We must rely on our common sense understanding of the world, our experience of other people, and the element of human trust. It follows that modern natural science cannot be our basic way of knowing, and the use of Occam's Razor to rule out principles that fall outside it is illegitimate.

Scientific method cannot deal with everything, and in particular does not deal well with:

• Things that are not quantitative, like the good, beautiful, and reasonable.

• Things that cannot be observed repeatedly, such as specific events in the past that leave no trace apart from memory.

• Things that are not observed by trained observers. Rogue waves, huge waves that suddenly appear at sea and often damage or sink ships, provide an example. For years, scientists denied their existence, in spite of abundant, clear, and convincing evidence to the contrary. The unpredictability and fleeting nature of the waves meant that the evidence was "anecdotal", that is, not based on controlled and repeatable observations by trained observers. Thus, it could not be taken into account in scientific discussions.

• Things, such as my own subjective experience, that cannot be observed at all by randomly chosen observers. Modern natural science has a big problem with consciousness, and so theoreticians of science often ignore it, deny its existence, or redefine it as something else. This takes denying the obvious to a whole new level. The movement that started with *cogito ergo sum* ends by denying consciousness.[4]

The result of these limitations of the scientific method is that scientific fundamentalists are unable to deal rationally and appro-

---

4 It seems inevitable that a strategy of understanding based on active, rational investigation of passive, mechanistic nature would have trouble accounting for the observer as part of nature. Oddities related to the position of the observer in the generally extremely successful theory of quantum mechanics provide a particularly vivid example of the difficulty. The Schrödinger cat paradox seems to show that, from the standpoint of quantum mechanics, a cat can be equally dead and not dead if both the cat and the event that might have killed it are shielded from observation.

priately with human and social reality. The problem is not merely theoretical. It means that, when scientism is applied to politics, decisions must be based on default assumptions like equality that trump good sense. Inclusiveness, "political correctness," and "zero tolerance" are based on a scientistic refusal to make distinctions, understand how things work, and rely on informal evidence that is fundamental to present-day political and moral thought. This is why people cannot get rid of these tendencies, no matter how stupid they think they are.

There are any number of other signs that basic understandings have gone wrong through principled rejection of good sense and other aspects of our normal way of understanding the world: the irrationalism of much modern thought, the coarseness and inhumanity of modern culture, the narrowness of many apologists for modern science, the abusiveness of discussions relating to religion and traditional morality, the ever-more-pervasive triviality and partisanship of our political life, and the replacement of discussion by censorship, which in much of the West is now backed by fines and imprisonment. To refuse to discriminate, to refuse to make decisions based on our experience of how systems work and what works best with them, is to promote all those consequences.

We have seen the future, and it has failed already. Why doubt that something so dysfunctional can be overcome? Undeserved success makes people stupid. This is especially true when the view that has won leaves out as much as scientism does. To say it is blinkered only hints at the depth of the problem. Rejection of formal and final cause, of essential features and modes of functioning, in favor of mechanism means that adherents of scientism cannot recognize what things are or what they are for without violating their own principles. Stupidity is thus a necessary consequence of taking their fundamental commitments seriously.

Problems with Liberalism

The problems of scientism are the problems of trying to do too much with too little. You cannot even begin to understand the world or deal with it reasonably, if you leave out qualities that cannot be measured and functional patterns that are lost in analysis of mechanism and unusual cases. Liberalism, which is a social and moral expression of scientism, has similar problems for similar reasons.

To begin, scientism does not let liberalism deal with questions of good and bad. Good and bad are not events in space, which means that the kind of reasoning favored by the natural sciences cannot deal with them. Liberals claim they do not need to do so. Their system lets a hundred flowers bloom, so that each of us can pursue his dream, regardless of his view of the good. The claim is obviously false. The "good" is whatever it is that makes a goal worth pursuing, and no man, government, or social order can stand above arguments about which goals are worth pursuing. Nor is it possible for government to make its goal the fulfillment of goals in general. One goal forecloses another. For example, the law cannot equally favor protecting the rights of the unborn and the right to choose abortion, and so it must decide which to prefer.

Liberals nonetheless want to treat goals equally and let people follow whichever ones they prefer. To make good on this aspiration, they have to do away with conflicting desires, since otherwise some people's goals will have to give way to those of others. Their solution is to tell us in effect that all goals are good and legitimate, but only if they can be integrated into a universal, rational system of production, distribution, consumption, and control. Freedom then becomes the ability to choose arbitrarily among goods that the system finds equally easy to handle. The result is that careers, consumer goods, and private indulgences that do not much affect other people are legitimate goals, while others, especially those that might restrict or demand something of other people, are not. Apart from the inhumanity of this limitation, which shuts out basic things like religion and family life that make life worth living, the line turns out to be hard to draw in practice. Careers compete with careers, rock music with peace and quiet, and offroad vehicles with unspoiled nature, not to mention that private indulgences like drugs and pornography have public effects that some people object to. In such cases, which goals are legitimate and which are oppressive?

If distinctions as to substantive value are out of bounds, it is hard to say. At bottom, equal freedom has too little content to give sensible answers to questions it must resolve, if it is to serve as the supreme principle of political life. Why should smoking be a forbidden vice, alcohol a tolerated indulgence, and sodomy a basic human right? Liberalism cannot say, except by appealing to standards of equality and efficiency that tell us very little. In default of other more appropriate standards, it can only consult administrative convenience and its own consistency and power. For this reason, its highest goal becomes not freedom, but the cause of freedom, the freedom to be a liberal and live in a way that supports liberalism. So a system of liberal equal freedom declares that a woman is free to have children with her same-sex partner by *in vitro* fertilization and then gives her the right to put the child in day care, but does not allow her to have a child within a traditional marriage. The former goals rely only on technology, bureaucracy, and the market, which are acceptable liberal institutions, while the latter requires marriage to be recognized as a specific institution with a natural function that deserves general social recognition and support. Its recognition would in consequence require unacceptable non-liberal understandings that put some people at a disadvantage. Even the very proposal of such a goal would oppress some people already, since it would pose a threat to their equal position to which other people are not subjected. For this reason, the goal must be rooted out and even its advocacy suppressed.[5]

To advance the cause of freedom, then, conduct, attitudes, and relationships must be supervised, controlled, and utterly transformed[6] in a way that excludes the things people actually want

---

5 See Desai, Chugh, and Brief, "Marriage Structure and Resistance to the Gender Revolution in the Workplace," on married male employees with stay-at-home wives as a threat to women's freedom and equality.

6 Consider, for example, Article 5 of the Convention on the Elimination of All Forms of Discrimination against Women, which requires parties to

take all appropriate measures . . . to modify the social and cultural patterns of conduct of men and women, with a view to achieving the elimination of prejudices and customary and all other practices which are based . . . on stereotyped roles for men and women.

So international law now requires governments to root out the view that men most. This is a situation indistinguishable from slavery. Man does not live by career, consumption, and private indulgences alone, and reducing everything to individual preference leaves no place for the goods he loves most. The attempt to abolish oppression thus ends in a militant and intolerant movement that tries to control everything for the sake of goals that are at odds with human nature. The politically correct welfare state is the "left wing" version of that movement, the Iraq war and "global democracy" the "right wing" version. Why should someone who favors actual freedom and humanity favor either?

Dropping the question of the good in favor of equal freedom seemed a way to avoid insoluble conflicts and facilitate human cooperation and flourishing. It was intended to put an end to religious violence and oppression. Instead, it sets up a new, perverse, destructive, and infinitely intolerant religion. The proponents of this religion do not put their view that the good is equal satisfaction of individual desire on a par with the views of other people, but feel called upon to force it on everyone everywhere. They consider equal freedom the self-evident highest moral principle and everything else irrational, oppressive, and violent. If you reject it, you are "extremist" or "divisive." They use these terms instead of "heretical" and "schismatic," but it means the same thing, the upshot being that you have to be shut up.

Catholicism and Islam have normally allowed adherents of other religions to raise their children in their own faith. In contrast, a common liberal objection to homeschooling is that it sometimes fails to inculcate what is called "tolerance," that is, acceptance of maximum equal preference satisfaction as the highest social standard. Tolerant multiculturalism turns out to be more intolerant than the supposedly intolerant theocracies of the past.[7]

and women differ in any way that matters. This is freedom and enlightenment?

7 For examples, see Hennessey, "The Freedom to Homeschool." According to the Supreme Court of Germany, the purpose of their general ban on homeschooling is to "counteract the development of religious and philosophically motivated parallel societies." Farris, "Banning Homeschooling Does Not Violate Rights."

A New World of Reason

We have seen that liberal modernity is a manifestation of intellectual modernity and thus of the modern conception of reason. To deal with our situation, we need a different and broader conception of reason that identifies sources of knowledge beyond modern natural science. Otherwise, objections to scientism and liberalism will go nowhere, and nothing their opponents say will make sense to anyone, not even, in the long run, themselves.

Good Sense

One way to start is to point out that knowledge requires good sense. We must rely on our own, but cannot demonstrate it, and so we must rely on others to confirm it and give us solid grounds for confidence we are right. It follows that knowledge has an essential dimension that is personal, social, and non-demonstrable.

Descartes tried to avoid the problem by claiming he could take good sense for granted. In the very first sentence of his *Discourse on Method* he says that:

> Good sense is, of all things among men, the most equally distributed: for every one thinks himself so abundantly provided with it, that those even who are the most difficult to satisfy in everything else, do not usually desire a larger measure of this quality than they already possess.

It is a very amusing quotation, but Descartes meant it literally and had to mean it literally. His system of universal, clear knowledge based on individual, subjective experience cannot work, unless he discounts personal good sense as an issue.

In fact, good sense cannot be assumed or discounted. It is subtle, complex, and hard to assess, and our need for it is all-pervasive. Some of us have more of it than others, and none has enough. The realization that we ourselves lack it is normally taken to be the beginning of wisdom. The kind of reasoning Descartes was willing to recognize, which Pascal called *l'esprit de géométrie* ("the mathematical mind"), and which insists on complete order, clarity, and certainty, is therefore not enough. We also need Pascal's *esprit de finesse* ("the intuitive mind"), a form of rea-

soning equivalent to what I call good sense and John Henry Newman calls the "illative sense." However named, it is what enables
us to draw reliable conclusions from myriad considerations we
could not possibly explain with any clarity or often even identify.

Tradition

So what is Pascal's *esprit de finesse* and where do we get it? In large
part, it is a matter of noticing and understanding what is going on
around us, that is, of recognizing the functional patterns that
order our world and how they can be expected to work in particular cases. Good sense thus involves the ability to see the world
as ordered by patterns directed toward ends that are innate to the
world itself and not added on by us to a world that can be fully
described as a system of blind material causation. It requires a
world that makes sense and so a world that is larger than the
world of modern natural science. The necessity of good sense is
thus a refutation of scientism.

The ability to recognize patterns correctly and understand
their implications is no doubt an inborn gift to some extent, but
it needs to be developed. As the skill of skills, it cannot be taught
directly. It deals with aspects of reality that cannot be clearly for-
mulated, so that it would be surprising if it could be made completely clear itself. The most important way we develop it is
through experience, dealing with whatever life throws up and
seeing what works, what does not, and what comes into focus
from all we do and suffer.

If we are ordinarily well-disposed, experience makes us wiser
as we grow older. Nonetheless, we are limited beings, life is
short, and the world is complex and subtle, so our own experience cannot tell us everything we need to know. That is one reason man is social and relies on social experience, or tradition, as
basic to what he is and does. Every complex activity has a tradition. Tradition is necessary to the very language by which we
articulate and order our thought, and without it life would
remain at an animal level. Modern natural science, which is
thought so strictly rational, is also traditional and even involves
an element of personal apprenticeship, inasmuch as, among scientists, it matters whom one trained under.

We thus have a source for the informal knowledge that enables us to recognize how things work and to evaluate goals, in order to decide what they are worth. That source is tradition. Everyone relies on it, and so everyone must admit its authority.

Revelation

Which tradition, though? There are many of them. Those that endure through a variety of changes normally have a great deal in common, since the accumulation of experience restrains oddities and brings out the basic features of things, but they differ on large points and small. Also, every tradition has inner conflicts, confusions, and disputed issues. Therefore, to say tradition is an authority seems to say very little. Even liberalism has a tradition, which demonstrates that we need to know which traditions to accept and which to avoid.

As a practical matter, the problem is rarely pressing. We all lead lives that are more or less ordered by attitudes and habits we share with others. We cannot do otherwise. Thus, we all recognize the authority of some tradition or other that is coherent enough for everyday purposes. The real question is what to do, when some feature of our own tradition comes to seem troubling or when a conflict arises with another tradition. There is no uniform answer to this question. Traditions normally maintain loyalty and deal with conflicts in their own way. Still, the answer to problems within and between traditions cannot always be more tradition. Tradition is valuable, because it helps us deal with life and the world. We have, moreover, a direct and personal interest in such things that trumps all traditions. So the question sometimes forces itself on us as to which tradition we should prefer or which way to develop our own, when life throws up a question tradition does not answer.

To a large extent, the question is one to be answered by Pascal's intuitive mind and Newman's illative sense: follow the direction that seems truest or best, given our best understanding and all the particulars. Still, there are principles that apply generally. When we consider what direction to take, we try to avoid problems. Thus, we should prefer traditions and developments of tradition that are not self-defeating. This rules out scientism and liberalism right away, since their insistent demand for comprehensive, perspicuous rationality, not to mention more recent developments like multiculturalism, rules out principled reliance on any tradition, even themselves.

The tradition we choose should also be one that is not doomed to fall apart. This standard is more demanding than it might seem. Tradition by itself has certain weaknesses. It can be wrong, but that is not the real problem, since it is reasonable to suppose that, if experience misleads us, then more experience is the best thing to set us straight. A more basic problem is that, by itself, tradition—the simple accumulation of experience and what various people connected to us have said and done—cannot resolve all the issues life throws up. Time reveals all things, including hidden conflicts in our ways of thinking and acting. Discussion and the passage of time do not in fact lead to consensus on all disputed matters.[8] Sometimes we can just agree to disagree, but not always, since enduring complex social cooperation depends on how we come out on basic matters. If people lack a common sense of what truth and honesty involve or a shared understanding of the ultimate purpose of common efforts, cooperation becomes less and less reliable.

It follows that tradition needs an authority transcending itself to resolve basic issues it cannot resolve on its own. Without such an authority, it will eventually become incoherent, and thought and reason, which depend on tradition, will fall into radical disarray. Science has recourse to observation, which works well for objects in space, but not everything is an object in space. In law, the necessary authority is provided by a constitutional court, but law is man-made, while reality is not. On other issues, the continuing coherence of tradition also requires the possibility of authoritative appeal to something beyond inherited consensus and present-day discussions.

With regard to the basic nature of the world, it seems that ultimate authority would need to be equivalent to revelation, to something that discloses the nature of things in a way that exceeds our own powers of investigation and reasoning. If no

---

8 As the liberal thinker, John Rawls, notes. Rawls, *Political Liberalism*.

such thing is available, we can no longer rely on tradition, since we know in advance it will not be able to resolve the basic issues life will eventually throw up. Since we know it is not going to develop in accordance with its own principles, but rather eventually fall apart, we cannot rationally believe what it tells us. Since we cannot trust in it, and since connected thought and belief must be integrated with some particular tradition, we cannot rationally believe in anything that is at all complicated or susceptible to dispute. Our lives, at least at the higher levels, become fundamentally irrational.

In summary, then, without a coherent tradition worthy of rational belief, reason and knowledge fall apart. Without some reliable way to resolve questions that cannot otherwise be resolved, no such tradition can exist. We cannot get by without something very much like an authoritative Church that is able to make decisions on questions that resist practical solution and will not go away. Something like a pope and *extra ecclesiam nulla salus* seem fundamental to a life in accordance with reason.

10

Making It Real

Everyone in public life today agrees that the law should root out the tendency to take sex, ethnicity, religion, and cultural background into account in forming connections that have practical importance. The main difference of opinion is between hardline conservatives who insist on applying this principle literally and categorically and moderates and liberals who say that specially favorable treatment for women and minorities is needed to eradicate stubborn patterns of discrimination. There is also a difference between progressives and moderates who want to add sexual orientation to the list of forbidden distinctions and a shrinking group of foot-draggers who resist the change.

Difficulty of the Struggle

There is no reason to take sides in a dispute over the fine points of a bad theory. Both parties' views are based ultimately on a technological understanding of reason and social order that insists that markets and expert bureaucracies are the only institutions with legitimate authority and that turns traditional classifications into arbitrary constructions. We have explored the inhumanity and destructiveness of such an outlook. What is needed is to get rid of it.

This is a difficult task. When people complain about inclusiveness, the effect is to alarm governing elites and make them redouble their efforts. If writers cast doubt on it, the solution is an informal system of censorship.[1] If popular referenda stand in

---

1 That seems to have been the main result of the publication of Herrnstein and Murray, *The Bell Curve: Intelligence and Class Structure in American Life*.

its way, judges throw out the results or administrators ignore or circumvent them.[2] And media attitudes make opposition unthinkable for elected officials. Liberal politicians support inclusiveness automatically, and conservatives who aspire to respectability must support it as well. The latter are under suspicion. Their positions offer fewer direct benefits to minorities and women and often include some sort of attachment to a traditional order that was non-inclusive. So conservatives are presumptively anti-minority, anti-woman, and anti-gay and must constantly demonstrate their inclusivist *bona fides* without ever persuading anyone. Their situation is quite unfair, since they accept the principles of the public order and quite generally choose inclusiveness over conservatism in case of conflict. Liberals' instincts are nonetheless sound, since to resist a totalitarian system on any point is in principle to reject it *in toto*. Mainstream conservatism is possible only through confusion.

In any case, it is unclear what sort of opposition to inclusiveness would make sense to people. Educated people now view themselves as citizens of a cosmopolitan society in which sexual, religious, and ethnic distinctions play no legitimate role except in very limited private settings. This outlook is absolutely basic among mainstream institutions and opinion leaders. It spreads and grows stronger with every generation and is especially strong among white people with economic and social aspirations.[3] To oppose inclusiveness, therefore, requires a view of how the world works that is wholly at odds with current assumptions. To take

2 See Romer v. Evans, 517 U.S. 620 (1996), which invalidated Proposition 2, an attempt to keep Colorado localities from making homosexuals a protected class for purposes of antidiscrimination laws; "CA's Anti-Immigrant Proposition 187 Is Voided, Ending State's Five-Year Battle with ACLU, Rights Groups," for events leading to California's abandoning the defense of Proposition 187, which tried to keep illegal aliens from using health care, public education, and other social services in California; and Mac Donald, "Elites to Anti-Affirmative-Action Voters: Drop Dead," for the administrative sabotage of Proposition 209, which barred affirmative action in California.

3 For survey results, see Guhname, "There Is No Silent but Sensible HBD Majority"; Guhname, "Are Attitudes Changing on IQ and Race?"; Guhname, "Political Moderation Shrinks as Years of Schooling Grow."

such a view not only injures a man socially and professionally, but makes him incomprehensible. What point could there be in going down such a path? Traditional discriminations are at home in a society that accepts informal habits, networks, and expectations as relevant to social order. By rejecting their relevance and depriving discriminations of a recognized function, modern ways of thinking make them seem arbitrary and malicious.

Antidiscrimination laws are as much a symptom as cause of our current disorders. If they were changed, other influences, such as the mass media, the welfare state, and the educational system, would still disrupt networks of informal customary connections. Since this is the case, what sense can there be in opposing them? Immigration, electronics, cheap travel, and global culture and commerce have done their work. Your next-door neighbor, your children's classmates, and your colleagues may have been born on another continent. Even if they were born a few blocks away, their ways of thought have been formed by electronic networks with no relation to heritage or geography, and by years of formal education and popular culture that tell them that particularity is bad, except as an exotic curiosity or way of debunking a substantive public order. Under such circumstances, how much relevance can inherited ways have?

Toward an Anti-Inclusivist Right

When a tendency has gone to extremes, it is most evident that something needs to be done to oppose it. Opposing one aspect of it may not be enough to reverse the tendency as a whole, but that is no reason to give up. The liberal attempt to rationalize society on neutral utilitarian lines is unsustainable and must be defeated, so that a form of society that makes human sense can once again establish itself. Instead of a free, equal, rational, and efficient society, that is, society understood as a machine for producing and distributing satisfactions, our goal should be a society that functions well in the way societies normally function.

Such a society would necessarily rely on particular traditions as ordering principles, along with the boundaries, exclusions, and authoritative attachments needed for them to function. It would thus take into account basic features of human life that accepted views ignore:

- Goods are largely social, since what is on offer and what it is worth depends largely on other people. For this reason, a purely individualistic approach to human life makes no sense.

- Nor does subjectivity as to values make sense. Viewing a choice as good includes the belief that it would be right to choose it, so that goods must be understood as objective.

- Knowledge, especially practical knowledge, is largely local and inarticulate and cannot be made otherwise. It is found distributed among the people at large and comes from the growth through experience of habits and perceptions that work.

- More generally, society learns through the development of tradition, and, as social beings, we learn and become able to function through participation in the traditions of our society.

- Traditions differ, since they arise locally in response to events and the situation, goals, and qualities of those involved. It follows that the attempt to bring about perfect rationality and uniformity by overriding the diversity of local traditions and connections destroys local knowledge in the form in which it actually exists and so plunges us into stupidity and brutality.

The effect of such recognitions is fundamental rejection of liberal modernity. Expert knowledge, social engineering, and the satisfaction of individual desire are not enough for a tolerable way of life. Thus, expertise, utility, and equal freedom cannot be final standards. When treated as such, their demands expand without limit and crowd out the goods people find most worthy of devotion. Other principles are also needed, along with the institutions, hierarchies, and distinctions that make it possible for them to function. This means that inclusiveness, which specifically aims at the abolition of such non-liberal hierarchies and distinctions, must be abandoned.

The point of getting rid of it is not favoring one group over another, but allowing functional systems of cooperation to reestablish themselves. We are social beings who carry on our lives in complex patterns that are mostly particular and local. We understand the world through these patterns and understand others as participants in them, that is, by reference to connections and roles. Stereotypes are therefore natural for us. The world that brings us forth shapes us in patterned ways that fit us for participation in its functioning. That is how we become what we are, and that is why it is normally good sense to prefer the patterns to which we are accustomed. It is natural to have different expectations regarding CEOs, day laborers, Harvard graduates, and graphic designers. Each has characteristic connections, functions, and roles, and so we think it natural to deal with them differently. Similarly, it is natural to expect somewhat different things of men and women, Frenchmen and Chinese. The reason is not that we hate and fear men and Frenchmen or women and Chinese, but that the natural and social differences of the sexes and historically-shaped differences of peoples and their cultures relate to functional patterns.

Sex roles, ethnicity, religious distinctions, and the like are less oppressive than liberating. They free us from formlessness and enable us to live with other people in a definite and functional manner that is, as much as possible, in accordance with our innate and acquired characteristics. In contrast, inclusiveness tends toward tyranny. In place of a largely self-governing equilibrium based on shared ways of life and natural, accustomed, or voluntary connections, it gives us an imposed social scheme based on money and bureaucratic hierarchy, in which we are manipulated through incentives and penalties or simply told what to do.

Fundamental Needs

To all appearances, inclusiveness could be abolished quite simply by a deep reduction in the scope of antidiscrimination laws.[4]

---

4 Such laws might, for example, be limited to transitory connections like hotel accommodations, while excluding relations like employment that are more complex, enduring, and basic to social functioning. Or rules like the demand for proportionality that force institutions to adopt quotas might be abolished, and those that remain might be limited to large institutions that are pervasively bureaucratic in any event.

However, it is part of a much larger system of social functioning, and people see it as fundamental, so that getting rid of it is not so easy. How would people respond to repeal of compulsory inclusiveness? How would they understand it? How could they be brought to support it? And if they need something other than technocratic thinking to understand it correctly, what will that be?

Ideals

The design of a better society cannot be decided in advance in all its details. What is needed is to start with the right basic understandings. If those are correct, then people will resolve specific issues implicitly and naturally through how they act in daily life. To go beyond liberalism, then, those who see its flaws need to make issues as basic as the good, beautiful, and true explicit as issues and propose a better understanding of them. A better world would arise quite naturally out of such an understanding, just as the world of liberal modernity arose out of the rejection of the qualitative and transcendent in favor of the numerical and practical that was pioneered in the early modern period by men such as Descartes and Bacon.

THE TRUE

The demand for inclusiveness is entangled with the problem of knowledge. Modernity makes man the measure and wants us to assert as true only the very little that we can demonstrate by formal logic and our own immediate experience. In particular, logic and immediate experience cannot demonstrate that classifications are correct, so modernity tells us we should treat them as something we make up for our own purposes rather than objective realities. Hence the current attitude toward discrimination and related matters. Human distinctions are considered acts of the will, and, if they turn to someone's disadvantage, they are construed as acts of aggression. To treat Tom, Dick, and Harry as different from oneself or each other in some determinate way is an exercise of the will of the classifier that says nothing about Tom, Dick, or Harry as they are in themselves. To act as if it does denies their equal humanity, since it denies that each is his own measure and makes his own equally-valid classifications for his own purposes.

This view of things is not often stated so baldly, but it lies behind the pervasive sense that there is something wrong with classifying human beings and noting human differences. To get beyond inclusiveness, then, we must get beyond views that make man the measure. As a rational matter, this should not be difficult, since there are very strong reasons to reject such views. A basic problem with them is that they cut us off from the world. We do not create ourselves or the world in which we live. Thus, we cannot understand ourselves or our situation if we put ourselves at the center and make ourselves the measure. Reality must be our standard, and we cannot connect with it, unless how things are, that is to say, their qualities and therefore their proper classification, is a knowable feature of things themselves rather than something we project onto them.

To engage the world and acquire knowledge, then, our thought must recognize standards beyond itself and go beyond what can be demonstrated from immediate experience and formal logic. That "going beyond" is part of what is called faith. There is always a gap between a proposition and the evidence for it, and faith is what bridges that gap. For this reason, faith is basic to knowledge and rationality. Since it is necessary to rationality, it should not be blind or arbitrary, but rather a rational faith that arises out of insight and experience. If it is to take into account the insight and experience of many men and generations, it must be part of a tradition, and, if the tradition is to be stable and reliable, it must be anchored in revelation. The modern revolution, which was an attempt to make man independent of tradition and revelation, therefore fails. As we discussed in the last chapter, knowledge and rationality depend on both.

But how, in a skeptical and scientistic world, can a better understanding of knowledge, reason, faith, and reality once again become available as a practical matter? How can it become part of the understandings that guide social functioning? To some extent, the modern world is doing the work for us. As time goes on, the practical and intellectual consequences of scientism and man-the-measure make it ever more evident that these views go nowhere. Postmodernism is one obvious expression of the will-fulness and radical skepticism to which modernity leads. What we need to do is clarify what has led to such a situation and what must be done to get out of it. To do so in an organized and reliable way requires a reform of education. This is a large effort, but we could start by studying thinkers such as Pascal, Burke, and Newman, who have dealt clearly and articulately with the inadequacies of modern understandings of knowledge and reason and how to go beyond them. Such thinkers, along with pre-modern thinkers like Plato and Aristotle, should therefore become integral to higher education, so that a broader and deeper understanding of life and thought can become part of the common sense of those who run things.

THE BEAUTIFUL

For modernity, beauty is no less a problem than truth. Since it makes man the measure, the scientistic view assimilates beauty to personal preference. It puts beauty in the eye of the beholder, and so makes pushpin as good as poetry. Such a view is contrary to all intelligent experience. Beauty is evidently part of how things are. It forces itself on us as something of indubitable value that cannot be reduced to personal preference. That is what it means to recognize it as beauty. Our perception of it may depend on taste, but a personal element does not make a perception merely subjective any more than the dependence of knowledge on qualities such as intelligence, experience, and good sense makes truth merely subjective.[5]

Beauty falsifies the dogma that denies reality to whatever is difficult to analyze and impossible to measure. It connects the material world to something beyond itself and gives us an immediate perception of something transcendent that is worthy of our love. It gives pleasure, so it attracts and pleases, but it is no less at odds with the technological outlook than fasting and prayer. It cannot

---

5 For a ground-breaking study of the objectivity of aesthetic value by a scientifically-trained architectural theorist, see Alexander, *The Nature of Order: An Essay on the Art of Building and the Nature of the Universe.*

be forced, and technique serves it, but does not create it. You have to wait on it and let it be what it is.

So anti-technocratic education must emphasize the beautiful. When those who appeal to tradition and the transcendent lack a sense of beauty, what they propose seems less an absorbing way of life that leads us to a grasp of the reality of things than one arbitrary ideology among others, a matter of rules, team spirit, and group dominance and not much else.

THE GOOD AND JUST

"The good" is whatever it is that makes a goal a rational object of choice. Every system, liberalism as much as any, promotes some choices over others and therefore proposes some goods as authoritative. Liberals define the good as getting what we want and justice as getting it equally, so that the point of politics and morality becomes a system of maximum equal preference satisfaction. We have explored the contradictions of that view in previous chapters.

For something better, we need a better understanding of what is good, that is to say, of what goals are most reasonable to pursue. Liberals do not want to discuss this question, because it suggests that law and policy should be based on a particular understanding of how to live, but the necessity of choosing makes it impossible to avoid. Liberalism itself holds that the most reasonable way to live is to pursue whatever one happens to want, as long as it fits a system that gives equal support to other people and their goals. This view has serious problems. It flattens out the good, since it makes what to pursue a simple matter of desire and manageability. And it fails to recognize goods that are not individual and transferable, since it makes justice consist of tallying up Tom, Dick, and Harry's goods and making the totals as equal as possible. The result is that the human good becomes very much like possession of a large sum of money, and justice like equalizing bank balances.

In fact, of course, the human good is far more complex, as well as being far more part of how we live, than liberalism assumes. When we are acting reasonably, we do not want particular things that we think are good so much as a good way of life. We want particular things, but only to the extent we see them as part of a way of life that we aspire to and believe we should aspire to, because it embodies a standard that seems worth living by. So the human good is not at all like having lots of money. Whether viewed from a commonsense, philosophical, or religious point of view, it is part of a whole way of life infused with qualities like truth and beauty that cannot be transferred or made to order.

Such a way of life requires more than the efforts of individuals, markets, and bureaucracies, the agencies liberalism accepts as legitimate and authoritative. Other social institutions, as well as the distinctions and disciplines they rely on, must provide a setting for complex non-economic goods and relationships. A society can only be good and just, if it helps the family be the family, communities be communities, the Church be the Church, and so on. Social justice is not a machine that delivers equal amounts of stuff to each of us and keeps us from interfering with each other, but a complex condition in which not only individuals but a variety of associations get what they need, so that each can make its contribution to human life. It is not equality, but paying each his due within a complex system of institutions and goods.[6]

That is a basic point distinguishing traditionalist thought, which takes the complexity of human life and its goods seriously, from the current view that makes a unified, rational, and efficient system for satisfying individual preferences the goal of political life. The former allows diversity and the discriminations and distinctions that order it and make it functional, while the latter flattens them out in the interests of clarity and control.

RELIGION

Social principles and cultural ideals do not hang in the air. To become reliable and concrete enough to order society, they need to be part of a more general understanding of man and the world. This understanding is the established religion of the society. Every society that is at all coherent has an established religion, which is to say an established understanding of the nature

---

6 See Catholic Church, *Catechism of the Catholic Church*, paragraph 1928.

of man, the world, and human obligation. As we have seen, inclusivist liberalism now holds such a position in the West.

We have also seen that inclusivist liberalism maintains itself by hiding its nature as a religion. The way beyond this impasse is to make the questions it suppresses explicit, so that the issue becomes which religion should win out. This is a complex issue from a political perspective. Practicalities are central to politics, and the first necessity for any establishment of religion is general agreement among serious and influential people that the world is more or less as the religion describes it. This means that, from the standpoint of political action, the initial public goals of those dissatisfied with the present establishment are likely to be quite modest. In America in 2013, they would include cutting back on the privileged position of inclusivist liberalism and insistence on a much broader conception of religious freedom and freedom of association as the basis for a *modus vivendi* among conflicting faiths and ways of life.

The concept of a *modus vivendi* is important. The question of Church, State, and minority rights has no final resolution, although liberals claim their own views offer one. Their views are a matter of simple reason, they say, which means that others can accept and live by them without violating the integrity of their own views to the extent those views are reasonable.[7] The solution seems fair to liberals, but there is no reason for anyone else to agree. Every universalism believes itself better founded than any other. Catholics believe their views are supported by reason. Muslims tend to be doubtful of reason as a guide, but claim support in God's final revelation. Why should either submit to the liberals? It is as easy for them as for liberals to say, "Each can do as he wants, as long as he accepts the rightful supremacy of our way of looking at things."

Under such circumstances, the conflict among competing views must be given a practical rather than theoretical solution. A *modus vivendi* among competing universalisms is usually possible, even though a non-controversial super-universalism that eliminates the possibility of basic conflict is not. No society is

---

7 See Rawls, *Political Liberalism*.

completely coherent. Its established religion may be more or less well-defined, and the nature and extent of its establishment can vary. Still, a *modus vivendi* among fundamental views that are basically in conflict is likely to be shifting and unstable, and some ideal regarding a religious establishment is necessary to guide action. Those who see the current order as destructive need to clarify their own goals and persuade each other as to what specific alternative is best and most workable in the long run. In that process, views that are better founded and work better will presumably do better. A discussion of what views those are will have to await another occasion.

A Favorable Setting

The good, beautiful, and true cannot be forced, and their effects are largely the result of organic, spontaneous growth.[8] Nonetheless, conscious action can promote the process. The growth and functioning of tradition require stability, decentralization, and limited government. Thus, a movement toward a less technocratic society must emphasize opposition to globalism, mass immigration, comprehensive schemes of social reform, and the all-competent administrative state. Specific institutions such as independent schools, religious communities, and economic undertakings are also needed to provide the setting for new growth in various ways:

- Traditional family life, supported by traditional sex roles and sexual morality, connects the individual and the social order. It makes people part of a network of families and institutions linked by common heritage and culture. It enables them to look after themselves without constant reliance on the state and so helps create a base from which new life can grow.

- Modern economic life has provided much of the impetus for the industrialization of social relations. The tendency toward

8 "The kingdom of God cometh not with observation." Luke 17:20. Also see Confucius, *The Doctrine of the Mean*: "Among the means for the regeneration of mankind, those made with noise and show are of the least importance."

radical rationalization is not likely to last forever. The decline of public loyalty and trust is likely to make large-scale impersonal economic arrangements less and less efficient and bring back older ones involving smaller enterprises and informal networks of trust that would necessarily be non-inclusive.

• Community always has some sort of religious basis. We recognize the authority of a community, when there is some principle that makes it part of what we are and directs it toward what we should be. For a community to maintain its own integrity over against a larger society of which it is part, and to which it is legally subject, its religious basis must be explicit and capable of maintaining boundaries. Examples can be drawn from the Jews, the early Church, the Mormons, and the pre-Vatican II Church in America.

• A way of life must be passed on to the next generation. This process is a responsibility of all social institutions, but some aspects of it belong particularly to the schools. The function of public and mainstream private schools today is to separate children from their parents' community and inculcate liberal modernity. Development of an independent system of education is a necessity for those who reject the direction of events.

In the years to come, a main political task of those attached to tradition and the transcendent will be protecting particular local communities in the face of a public order that demands uniformity and top-down transparency for the sake of comprehensive supervision and control.

Making the Case

But how do we persuade people that a different and better sort of society is possible and that traditionalist and transcendent principles are the way to get there, while inclusiveness and liberal modernity are not?

Inclusivism looks invincible at present, but its weaknesses are fundamental and eventually doom it. The key to overcoming inclusiveness is understanding. If we see liberalism as radically flawed and therefore vulnerable, we have a chance to be effective.

Otherwise, we are likely to give up and waste our efforts in complaints and recriminations. With that in mind, the first step is to disrupt and transform current ways of discussing politics, so that fruitful discussion once again becomes possible. In particular, we need to:

- Claim the right to define the problem. The point of politics is not abolition of inequalities and barriers to the free expression of the will, but rather it is the defense and facilitation of a life worth living. If you cannot talk about what that is, you cannot talk about politics.

- Reclaim history. It is not the story of human emancipation culminating in an ever more universal and comprehensive system of human rights. It is the story of attempts to deal with problems and attain goods, and, as such, it has its victories and defeats, very few of which are unequivocal or irreversible.

- Reclaim the normal and justify the inherited. People may question what is normal, but we cannot get along without the concept of normality, and tradition is necessary to establish what it means.

- Claim the high ground. We have little hope of achieving anything enduring, unless we connect our views to the common good. Opposing inclusiveness is not bigotry. Rather, it is support for what is normal and human, and we should be confident that the need for a normally functioning society can eventually be made evident to men of good will generally.

It is difficult to silence all discussion in modern society, especially given its stated preference for reason. This situation presents a host of opportunities. We live in a target-rich environment with a thousand forums in which to carry on the fight. Our goal is to present, in every possible setting, views that are better and more adequate than liberalism in terms others can understand. The liberal system is knit together so closely that questioning one part undermines all the others. The key is to keep raising issues in as many ways as possible, until they cannot be shrugged off, and others start raising them on their own.

If we are clear on fundamentals, we can confidently present our concerns, using whatever tactics seem prudent. Provocation is sometimes useful, but it is usually better to find common ground and try to show that what we propose is implicit in what others already believe. The key is to define the common ground correctly.

Rather than engaging liberals by accepting their stated principles, which lead back to scientism and liberalism, we should point out the real principles by which they live, which always smuggle in objective goods beyond the ones they recognize officially. Why, for example, are educated liberals so much more orderly in their private lives than their principle of valuing lifestyles equally would suggest?[9] And why do they idolize liberal heroes and martyrs, when liberal theory makes individual fulfillment the highest standard? It is evident that, like other people, liberals have standards beyond maximum preference satisfaction, and clarifying that point should make it possible to discuss what those standards are and what they should be. The good, beautiful, and true could then become once again a matter of serious discussion.

The left has made a practice of attacking the remnants of traditional order at their most vulnerable points. Anti-liberals need to reverse the practice. We must present an alternative clearly and forcefully, countering the Left's one-liners ("Freedom!" "Equality!" "Tolerance!" "Reason!") with comebacks of our own, backed by serious theories about man and the world. If we make the effort, people will get used to what we have to say, even if it seems outrageous at first, and it takes them a while to understand what it means. True believers are not likely to change their views, but their power depends on the acquiescence of those less committed. For this reason, our arguments are likely to have more effect than is apparent. If enough people do understand what we say, and it makes sense to them, the possibilities of public discussion and social order can change suddenly and radically. Until recently, it was the traditional order that was being subverted, and whoever was not with it was against it. Now it is the liberal order that is established, and whoever is shaky in supporting it favors its opponents.

---

9 For a discussion of the comparatively cautious lifestyles of elite Americans generally, see Murray, *Coming Apart: The State of White America*, 1960–2010.

Limits

It is worth noting that rejecting inclusiveness does not mean going to some opposite extreme. To admit a principle is not to exaggerate it. Limited government and localism do not, for example, mean no government. Government represses violence and protects property. It guards national boundaries and so establishes a stable setting for the complex of connections that constitutes a functional society. It supports and regularizes productive relationships, for example, by defining family and commercial law. Ideally, it also provides assistance and leadership in harmonizing the activities of various social authorities, so that they remain mutually supporting.[10]

Nor does decentralization mean indifference to the whole. Local communities have to be part of something larger, so that their standards can be seen to have objective validity and a higher end. And an overall framework is needed, so that intergroup relations do not degenerate into the rule of the strongest or war of all against all. The co-existence of multiple universalisms within the West makes that difficult, but politics is the art of the possible, and we must try to strike the best balance we can.

At a more theoretical level, we cannot talk about people without reference to their place in systems larger than themselves, so roles and stereotypes matter. Nonetheless, it remains true that people are more than their roles and individuals more than their relationships. Stereotypes, like other social ordering principles, have limits.

Modern thought insists on conceptual simplicity. It tends to create polarities and then suppress one of the poles. Sometimes it separates us radically from our roles and so from the relationships that define us. This tendency gave rise to Descartes' philosophy, with its radical opposition between the ego and the world. Today it convinces people that discrimination is simply irrational, since a man's roles and connections show nothing about what he

---

10 That is part of the Catholic concept of subsidiarity. How to coordinate and support social functioning without excess centralization is of course a difficult question under present circumstances.

is. A contrary modern tendency leads people to deny that a man is more than a collection of events and relationships. If he is more than that, skeptics ask, what more is he? It is hard to give an answer they will accept, so they insist we stick to what can be observed and measured, namely, events and patterns of events, and forget about substantial identities. In consequence, persons and things dissolve into a network of social and natural functions.

The result is a conflict between insistence on personal autonomy and a contrary insistence on the mechanistic aspects of life. Modern thought drives both to extremes, so that those who deny the absolute independence of man from his social connections are thought to deny the significance of the individual, while those who say the individual matters feel compelled to make his emancipation from roles and connections the highest human goal. The modern outlook thus oscillates between abolition of the individual and denial that he depends on his qualities and setting for what he is. There is obviously something wrong with such a situation. We need to follow a middle way that aligns with common sense and natural human tendencies, one that accepts that man is constituted by both individuality and relationships.

11

Conclusion

The future is hard to predict, and liberalism is adaptable. From seeming death, it has come back to life more than once. Still, nothing lasts forever. So how will it end?

Terminal Crisis

Life is full of unexpected turns, and what is impossible today is unavoidable tomorrow. Liberalism and inclusiveness depend on particular circumstances, and, when those circumstances vanish, so will they.[1] Inclusiveness is part of the liberal bubble, a gross overextension of a line of development assumed capable of going on forever. Bubbles burst, the dreams of youth dissipate, pride goes before destruction, and the world seems very different the morning after. Shock that the bubble burst is followed immediately by amazement that it lasted as long and went as far as it did.

Much of the strength of liberalism is its connection to the self-interest, self-understanding, and manner of functioning of particular institutions: expertise, bureaucracy, modern natural science, and modern commerce and industry. The aggressive imperialism of these institutions destroys other patterns of social life, so that people lose the ability to function apart from them. That seems to put those institutions in a very strong position, because it makes them indispensable.

On the other hand, the absolute dominance of such institutions and the consequent overthrow of traditional social patterns

---

1 For a more detailed account of how liberalism could be replaced by a quite different view, see Kalb, "After Liberalism: Notes Toward Reconstruction."

serve to destroy the habits of honesty, good faith, and reliability on which those very institutions depend. These circumstances also destroy the conditions that enable people to live happily and well. There are basic aspects of life that liberal institutions cannot deal with, and the lack of fit with human life makes them unlikely to retain the loyalty they need to survive. They do not deal well with family life, for example, and so liberals do not have children. Meanwhile, the future belongs to people who do.[2] Crude measures like surveys of charitable giving and reported happiness also suggest that liberalism offers its adherents a less social and less satisfying way of life than other possibilities.[3]

Liberalism, like all human things, will therefore come to an end. But how? A failing system can continue in form, while disappearing in substance, and that may be the most likely outcome of the current situation. If the inclusivist regime bogs down in its own corruption and incoherence, as seems likely, that could slow its self-destruction and allow time for other principles of order to re-establish themselves. It was the imperfections of the Soviet system that saved it for a time by allowing non-socialist arrangements like barter, private garden plots, and the black market to make up for the system's deficiencies and point the way to the future.

The same could happen with the current regime. Social and economic life always involves family connections and other informal networks of trust that are difficult to suppress. Such arrangements are anti-inclusive, since they are based on kinship and common background. They get things done, though, and are difficult to suppress or do without. The more they are attacked, the more close-knit they become. So they are likely to remain with

---

2 In general, liberals are considerably more likely to be unmarried, divorced, adulterous, cohabiting, and childless than conservatives. Guhname, "Liberals and Family." On the likelihood that the future belongs to the religious, see Kaufmann, *Shall the Religious Inherit the Earth?: Demography and Politics in the Twenty-First Century*; Longman, "The Global Baby Bust."

3 See Brooks, *Who Really Cares: The Surprising Truth About Compassionate Conservatism*, on charitable giving, and Brooks, *Gross National Happiness: Why Happiness Matters for America—and How We Can Get More of It*, on reported happiness.

us and allow the liberal system to maintain its form for a time, while functioning in a more and more non-liberal manner, and then survive it and become basic to the post-liberal order. Already we see a tendency toward dynasticism in American politics, and an emphasis on personal networking in businesses and professions where protective legislation and antidiscrimination rules have made formal recommendations and certifications unreliable. This tendency seems likely to extend itself and to grow through the increasing importance of non-Western ethnic groups who lack ingrained allegiance to liberal ideals.

Other exceptions to inclusiveness that may foreshadow the future and extend the life of the system at the expense of its rigorous consistency include religious communities and private education and homeschooling. Such arrangements involve self-segregation and should not exist at all in an inclusivist society. To allow life to go on, however, ideology often averts its gaze from what is actually happening. Family, religion, and independent education aid social functioning, and so it is practical to allow them to maintain themselves. The slogan of diversity can excuse failures to enforce inclusion and make room for those who want to carry on their own way of life independent of the principles publicly professed. In any event, liberalism prefers pressure and nagging to the direct use of force, which means that dedicated parents and communities can usually resist it. Local institutions based on family and religion are therefore likely to survive, at least in America, where they can appeal to ideals of local initiative and limited government.

It is likely, then, that the current regime will become less effective and consistent, while maintaining its official ideology. It will very likely tend toward a pattern common in ethnically diverse parts of the Third World: a radically divided society with little public life and a government that combines democratic and inclusivist rhetoric with tyranny, weakness, corruption, nepotism, and crony capitalism. Liberal inclusiveness would reign officially, but below the surface the real life of the society would be carried on through kinship, ethnic, religious, and criminal networks.

What Next?

Every tomorrow has another tomorrow. Chaos does not last forever, because people cannot live that way. Some principle will eventually create a new order that recognizes natural ways of human functioning and connects them to something higher.

A Rejuvenated Liberalism?

Liberalism and modernity seem too well defined and their logic too demanding for the present regime to evolve into something more adequate to human life, while remaining recognizably liberal and modern. Nonetheless, there are always ambiguities in established creeds and practices, and ambiguities can accumulate, grow, and eventually transform the situation in unexpected ways. So the possibility of a more humane and enduringly functional liberal modernity seems unlikely, but cannot be entirely excluded. In other words, the theory of liberalism presented in this book could be wrong or basically incomplete.

A More Radical Particularism?

European public life traditionally depended on general acceptance of a substantive universalism that allowed public discussion to be free, as well as focused. This universalism was initially Roman Catholic, but Catholic culture eventually gave way to cultural derivatives that became increasingly secular and dependent on ethnic and national culture. Hence the European nation-state, together with the conception of European or Western civilization.

The coherent, national cultures on which such arrangements rested depended on stable populations. Large-scale movements of peoples mostly stopped in Europe in the eighth century, and those who lived close together were able to develop common habits, understandings, and loyalties that allowed extensive systems of voluntary cooperation and trust to grow up and sustain themselves. The result was a European civilization composed of regions and nations. That stage of civilization now seems to have ended. Mass third-world immigration, multiculturalism, and the imperialism of commercial and bureaucratic institutions have disrupted inherited connections. Substantive public life has been replaced by public relations, propaganda, spin, and the cult of the expert. And, in any event, locality is much less important, when jet travel and electronics makes China almost as reachable as the next street.

The obvious result of the disappearance of substantive, public culture combined with ethnic and religious diversity is a Levantine form of society: no social trust, no public spirit, nonfunctional formal institutions, pervasive official corruption, nepotism, and self-seeking dynastic rule. One likely outcome of the New World Order can therefore be seen in the radically cosmopolitan and diverse (and hence radically particularist and inward turning) way of life that has long prevailed in the Cradle of Civilization. In America, the growing stupidity, dishonesty, and brutality of public discussion and the combination of anarchy and tyranny that is coming to pervade our political system suggest that we are headed in the same direction. Our political dynasties are still informal, and, instead of bazaars and walled city quarters, we have eBay, shopping malls, and gated communities, but how much difference is there? While we are trying to turn the Middle East into Iowa, Iowa is turning into the Middle East.

A Middle Eastern form of society is likely to have some popular appeal in comparison with inclusivist liberalism. For ordinary people, particularism offers meaning, purpose, community, and dignity in a world otherwise lacking these things. And its appeal to the gifted is likely to increase in the long run because of the increasing incoherence and degradation of secular, cosmopolitan culture. Those who do not belong to cohesive communities are likely to fall silent from lack of anything compelling or even coherent to say, or else die out from failure to reproduce or from disorders resulting from the failure to pass down a workable way of life. The intellectual future is likely to belong to new Augustines speaking from a point of view based on something much more concrete and much more open to the transcendent than Enlightenment reason.

A Universal Religion?

Particularism can never be absolute. Some overarching principle is needed to mitigate conflict and provide a general ground of justification, cooperation, and legitimate rule. In the Middle East, absence of intelligent public life has gone together with dominance by a simplified fanatical religion.[4] If the West becomes the Middle East, it may well go the same way. As always, extremes provoke their opposites. Scientism, liberalism, and inclusiveness lead to a radically cosmopolitan form of society that lacks an overall principle of connection and becomes radically divided and inward-turning. Some principle of ultimate connection and justification is nonetheless needed. That principle needs to combine a coherent notion of universality with the distinctiveness and the ability to attract loyalty of the tribalisms that have come to dominate social life. Islam has proved its ability to fill the gap.

That result is not inevitable. The Roman Catholic Church is the great opponent of extremes. Its doctrines of Creation and Incarnation, as well as its hierarchical and sacramental structure, reconcile particularity and universality, while its theology reconciles revelation and public reason. This combination of qualities made Europe what it has been and gave it the unity in diversity that enabled it to turn the tide against Islam in Sicily, Crete, and Spain, and at Tours, Lepanto, and Vienna. If this is so, then the issue for the future is whether the Church can pull itself together, revert to type, and revitalize the West.

The prospect seems unlikely, given the present state of the West and the Church. Still, we live in an age of dissolution from which no one seems exempt. Islam and liberal thought have at least as many problems as Catholicism. There is a race to the bottom, but not everyone can lose, comebacks do happen, and the superiority of basic principle eventually tells. The initial triumph of Christianity came, when paganism could no longer support social cohesion or sustain intellectual life, and first the state and then the best thinkers became Christian. The same could happen again. In the end, whatever is best founded, whatever has the best account of life and the world and the most intelligent and flexible scheme of authority, will have the best chance of dealing effectively with the complications life keeps throwing up. We shall see.

4 For a discussion of the irrationalist tendencies in Islam, see Reilly, *The Closing of the Muslim Mind: How Intellectual Suicide Created the Modern Islamist.*

Prospects

How we think things will end depends on what we think is true. Liberalism seems all-powerful, but it leaves out too much. It claims to solve all problems and has the support of all respectable authority, but it is based on obvious falsehoods and strikes at the root of social functioning and human happiness. It cannot last. Brussels functionaries are not going to show us the pathway to the future.

When established views and institutions do not establish the conditions for a good way of life, people will look for something better. We will offer them what they need, if we live well ourselves and are able to explain how we do so and why it makes sense. We cannot expect fast results, but, if we have something to offer, we have reason to be confident in the ultimate outcome. Basic issues cannot be suppressed forever and can reassert themselves very quickly, when the wind changes. Pour water into a bucket full of sand, and it looks as if nothing is happening, until the bucket overflows.

The question is how we should live now and what there will be in place to pick up the pieces left by the ultimate disintegration of liberalism. The fall of communism in Russia has meant mafia rule and the collapse of life expectancies. We should hope things do not go so badly in the liberal West and that we can do better, when the present order falls apart. Our task is to prepare for that day and live well in the meantime. The more we have thought the issues through and the better the available alternatives, the better things will go for ourselves and for our children and country.

Bibliography

"AL." "EEOC Files Suit Over Use of Credit and Criminal Histories in Hiring." *Workplace Prof Blog*, December 1, 2009. http://lawprofessors.typepad.com/laborprof_blog/2009/12/eeoc-files-suit-over-use-of-credit-and-criminal-histories-in-hiring.html.

Alexander, Christopher. *The Nature of Order: An Essay on the Art of Building and the Nature of the Universe*. Berkeley, CA: The Center for Environmental Structure, 2002.

Allen, Charlotte. "Science Quotas for Women–A White House Goal." *Minding the Campus*, July 7, 2012. http://www.mindingthecampus.com/forum/2012/07/when_college_women_studyscienc.html.

Allen, Douglas W., Catherine Pakaluk, and Joseph Price. "Nontraditional Families and Childhood Progress Through School: A Comment on Rosenfeld." *Demography* (n.d.): 1–7. Accessed January 30, 2013. doi:10.1007/s13524-012-0169-x.

Angeles, Luis. "Children and Life Satisfaction." *Journal of Happiness Studies* 11, no. 4 (2010): 523–538.

Aquinas, Thomas. "Summa Theologica, Second Part of the Second Part, Question 101, Article 1." In *Summa Theologica*, 2011. http://www.newadvent.org/summa/3101.htm#article1.

———. "Summa Theologica, Second Part of the Second Part, Question 26, Articles 6–8." In *Summa Theologica*, 2011. http://www.newadvent.org/summa/3026.htm#article6.

Auster, Lawrence. "Non-Islam Theories of Islamic Extremism." *View from the Right*, October 19, 2007. http://www.amnation.com/vfr/archives/009044.html.

———. "Refusing to Say That Muslim Terrorists Are Muslims." *View from the Right*, June 4, 2006. http://www.amnation.com/vfr/archives/005799.html.

———. "The Truth of Interracial Rape in the United States." *FrontPageMag.com*, May 3, 2007. http://archive.frontpagemag.com/readArticle.aspx?ARTID=26368.

Baker, Al. "In One School, Students Are Divided by Gifted Label—and Race." *The New York Times*, January 12, 2013, sec. Education. http://www.nytimes.com/2013/01/13/education/in-one-school-students-are-divided-by-gifted-label-and-race.html.

Baldwin, Steve. "Child Molestation and the Homosexual Movement." *Regent University Law Review* 14 (2002): 267–282.

Berger, Eric. "English Linked to Promiscuity in Hispanic Teens." *Houston Chronicle*, March 8, 2005. http://www.chron.com/news/houston-texas/article/English-linked-to-promiscuity-in-Hispanic-teens-1942500.php.

Berggren, Henrik, and Lars Trägårdh. "The Nordic Way: Social Trust and Radical Individualism," 2010. http://www.globalutman-ing.se/wp-content/uploads/2011/01/Davos-The-nordic-way-fi-nal.pdf.

Berthoud, Jean-Marc. "The Bible and the Nations, Part 1." *Calvinism Today* 3, no. 4 (1993): 4–8.

———. "The Bible and the Nations, Part 2." *Calvinism Today* 4, no. 1 (1994): 12–16.

———. "The Bible and the Nations, Part 3." *Calvinism Today* 4, no. 2 (1994): 20–24.

Bertonneau, Thomas F. "The Apocalypse of Modernity." *The Brussels Journal*, June 18, 2012. http://www.brusselsjournal.com/node/4953.

Block, Walter. *The Case for Discrimination*. Auburn, AL: Ludwig von Mises Institute, 2010.

Bolce, Louis, and Gerald de Maio. "Our Secularist Democratic Party." *The Public Interest* (Fall 2002): 3–21.

Bookbinder, Paul. "Weimar Germany: The Republic of the Reasonable." 101. Manchester University Press, 1996.

Bradley, Gerard V. "Academic Integrity Betrayed." *First Things* (September 1990).

Brand, Christopher, Denis Constales, and Harrison Kane. "Why Ignore the G Factor—Historical Considerations." Accessed January 11, 2013. http://bussorah.tripod.com/nyborg.html.

Breslau J, Borges G. "Migration from Mexico to the United States and Conduct Disorder: A Cross-national Study." *Archives of General Psychiatry* 68, no. 12 (December 1, 2011): 1284–1293. doi:10.1001/archgenpsychiatry.2011.140.

Bronson, Po, and Ashley Merryman. "See Baby Discriminate." *Newsweek*, September 14, 2009. http://www.newsweek.com/id/214989.

Brooks, Arthur C. *Gross National Happiness: Why Happiness Matters for America—and How We Can Get More of It*. New York: Basic Books, 2008.

———. *Who Really Cares: The Surprising Truth About Compassionate Conservatism*. Basic Books, 2007.

Brooks, David. "The Opportunity Gap." *The New York Times*, July 9, 2012, sec. Opinion. http://www.nytimes.com/2012/07/10/opinion/brooks-the-opportunity-gap.html.

"CA's Anti-Immigrant Proposition 187 Is Voided, Ending State's Five-Year Battle with ACLU, Rights Groups." *American Civil Liberties Union*. Accessed January 30, 2013. http://www.aclu.org/immigrants-rights/cas-anti-immigrant-proposition-187-voided-ending-states-five-year-battle-aclu-righ.

Bibliography

"California Institute of Technology Overview." *QuestBridge.* Accessed January 11, 2013. http://www.questbridge.org/caltech-overview.

Cameron, Paul. *Medical Consequences of What Homosexuals Do.* Family Research Institute. Accessed January 31, 2013. http://www.familyresearchinst.org/2009/02/medical-consequences-of-what-homosexuals-do/.

———. *The Psychology of Homosexuality.* Family Research Institute. Accessed January 31, 2013. http://www.familyresearchinst.org/2009/02/the-psychology-of-homosexuality/.

Caplan, Bryan. "Good News and Bad News on Parenting." *The Chronicle Review,* January 23, 2009. http://chronicle.com/free/v55/i20/20b00501.htm.

Carter, Jimmy. "Former U.S. President Jimmy Carter's Remarks at the Funeral Service for President Gerald R. Ford." The Carter Center, January 3, 2007. http://www.cartercenter.org/news/editorials_speeches/ford_eulogy.html.

Catholic Bishops' Conference of England & Wales. *Diversity and Equality Guidelines.* London: Colloquium (CaTEW) Ltd, 2005. http://www.catholicchurch.org.uk/content/download/3738/25367/file/Feb2005_Diversity%20and%20Equality%20Guidelines.pdf.

Catholic Church. *Catechism of the Catholic Church.* Liguori, MO: Liguori Publications, 1994.

Charlton, Bruce. "The Story of Real Science." *The Story of Real Science,* August 10, 2010. http://thestoryofscience.blogspot.com/.

Chavez, Linda. "Latino Fear and Loathing." *Townhall,* May 25, 2007. http://townhall.com/columnists/LindaChavez/2007/05/25/latino_fear_and_loathing.

Chesterton, Gilbert Keith. "The Patriotic Idea." In *England: A Nation: Being the Papers of the Patriot's Club,* edited by Lucian Oldershaw, 1–43. R. Brimley Johnson, 1904.

Chomsky, Noam. *Understanding Power: The Indispensible Chomsky.* New York: The New York Press, 2002.

Ciotti, Paul. *Money And School Performance: Lessons from the Kansas City Desegregation Experiment.* Cato Policy Analysis. Cato Institute, March 16, 1998. http://www.cato.org/pubs/pas/pa-298.html.

Clark, Laura. "Three-year-olds Being Labelled Bigots by Teachers as 250,000 Children Accused of Racism," September 23, 2010. http://www.dailymail.co.uk/news/article-1314438.

Coates, Peter A. *American Perceptions of Immigrant and Invasive Species: Strangers on the Land.* University of California Press, 2006.

Cobb, Jonathan, and Richard Sennett. *The Hidden Injuries of Class.* New York: W.W. Norton & Company, 1993.

Cochran, G., J. Hardy, and H. Harpending. "Natural History of Ashkenazi Intelligence." *Journal of Biosocial Science* 38, no. 5 (2005): 659–693.

Cochran, Gregory, and Henry Harpending. *The 10,000 Year Explosion: How Civilization Accelerated Human Evolution.* New York: Basic Books, 2009.

Coffin, Shannen W. "Kagan's Abortion Distortion." *National Review Online,* June 29, 2010. http://www.nationalreview.com/blogs/print/243362.

Cohn, Bob. "21 Charts That Explain American Values Today." *The Atlantic,* June 27, 2012. http://www.theatlantic.com/national/archive/2012/06/21-charts-that-explain-american-values-today/258990/.

Conner, Laurene. "Social Teachings At Risk In The American Catholic Church." *The Forum Quarterly* IX, no. 3 (Fall 1996).

Cose, Ellis. *The Rage of a Privileged Class: Why Are Middle-Class Blacks Angry? Why Should America Care?* New York: Harper Perennial, 1994.

Craine, Patrick B. *Alberta Backtracks: Parents Can Teach Beliefs on Homosexuality, but Homeschoolers Still Concerned,* 2012. http://www.lifesitenews.com/news/alberta-gvmt-backtracks-parents-can-teach-gay-sex-is-a-sin-but-homeschooler.

————. "Ontario Education Minister: Catholic Schools Can't Teach Abortion Is Wrong—That's 'misogyny'." *LifeSiteNews,* October 10, 2012. http://www.lifesitenews.com/news/ontario-education-minister-catholic-schools-cant-teach-abortion-is-wrong.

D'Souza, Dinesh. *The End of Racism: Principles for a Multiracial Society.* New York: Free Press, 1995.

Dalrymple, Theodore. *In Praise of Prejudice: The Necessity of Preconceived Ideas.* New York: Encounter Books, 2007.

————. *Life at the Bottom.* Chicago: Ivan R. Dee, 2001.

De Dreu, C.K.W., L.L. Greer, M.J.J. Handgraaf, S. Shalvi, G.A. Van Kleef, M. Baas, F.S. Ten Velden, E. Van Dijk, and S.W.W. Feith. "The Neuropeptide Oxytocin Regulates Parochial Altruism in Intergroup Conflict Among Humans." *Science* 328, no. 5984 (June 10, 2010): 1408–1411. doi:10.1126/science.1189047.

Dean, Cornelia. "At a Scientific Gathering, U.S. Policies Are Lamented." *The New York Times,* February 19, 2006, sec. National. http://www.nytimes.com/2006/02/19/national/19science.html.

Deparle, Jason. "Two Classes in America, Divided by 'I Do'." *The New York Times,* July 14, 2012, sec. U.S. http://www.nytimes.com/2012/07/15/us/two-classes-in-america-divided-by-i-do.html.

Derbyshire, John. "The Husks of Dead Theories." *National Review Online,* April 24, 2009. http://article.nationalreview.com/?q=YjIwZTAwODBjNjZmNzRlMWViMDYwOTEwZDZhOWIyZWI=.

————. "The Talk: Nonblack Version." *Taki's Magazine,* April 5, 2012. http://takimag.com/article/the_talk_nonblack_version_john_derbyshire.

Desai, Sreedhari D., Dolly Chugh, and Arthur Brief. "Marriage Structure and Resistance to the Gender Revolution in the Workplace" (March 12, 2012). http://papers.ssrn.com/sol3/papers.cfm?abstract_id=2018259.

Diamond, Stanley. "Reversing Brawley." *The Nation,* October 31, 1988.

Dillon, Sam. "Officials Step Up Enforcement of Rights Laws in Education." *The New York Times*, March 8, 2010, sec. Education. http://www.nytimes.com/2010/03/08/education/08educ.html.

Dreher, Rod. "The Failures Of Integration." *The American Conservative*, December 6, 2012. http://www.theamericanconservative.com/dreher/the-failures-of-integration/.

Eberstadt, Mary. *Adam and Eve After the Pill: Paradoxes of the Sexual Revolution*. San Francisco: Ignatius Press, 2012.

Epstein, Richard. *Forbidden Grounds: The Case Against Employment Discrimination Laws*. Cambridge, MA: Harvard University Press, 1992.

Erbentraut, Joseph, and Joy Resmovits. "Chicago Public School Students Face Racial Discipline Gap: Education Department." *Huffington Post*, March 6, 2012. http://www.huffingtonpost.com/2012/03/06/chicago-public-schools-discipline-gap-education-department_n_1323681.html.

Esipova, Neli, and Julie Ray. *700 Million Worldwide Desire to Migrate Permanently*. Gallup, November 2, 2009. http://www.gallup.com/poll/124028/700-million-worldwide-desire-migrate-permanently.aspx.

Esolen, Anthony. "A College, of All Things." *Mere Comments*, March 4, 2007. http://touchstonemag.com/merecomments/2007/03/a_college_of_al/.

Estimates of Funding for Various Research, Condition, and Disease Categories (RCDC). National Institutes of Health, February 14, 2011. http://report.nih.gov/rcdc/categories/.

Farris, Michael. "Banning Homeschooling Does Not Violate Rights: U.S. Attorney General's Office | LifeSiteNews.com." *LifeSiteNews*. Accessed February 13, 2013. http://www.lifesitenews.com/news/banning-homeschooling-does-not-violate-rights-u.s.-attorney-generals-office.

Fausto-Sterling, Anne. *Sexing the Body*. New York: Basic Books, 2000.

Feldblum, Chai. "Moral Conflict and Liberty: Gay Rights and Religion." *Brooklyn Law Review* (2006).

Felluga, Dino. "Introductory Guide to Critical Theory," January 31, 2011. http://www.purdue.edu/guidetotheory/genderandsex/modules/butlergendersex.html.

Feser, Edward. "Stupak's Enablers?" *What's Wrong with the World*, March 29, 2010. http://www.whatswrongwiththeworld.net/2010/03/stupaks_enablers.html.

Finnis, John. "'Shameless Acts' in Colorado: Abuse of Scholarship in Constitutional Cases." *Academic Questions* 7, no. 4 (Fall 1994): 10.

Fleming, Bruce. "The Cost of a Diverse Naval Academy." *The Capitol (Annapolis, MD)*, June 14, 2009.

Franc, Michael. "Democrats Wake up to Being the Party of the Rich." *The Heritage Foundation*, November 6, 2007. http://www.heritage.org/research/commentary/2007/11/democrats-wake-up-to-being-the-party-of-the-rich.

Freeman, Derek. *Margaret Mead in Samoa: The Making and Unmaking of an Anthropological Myth*. Cambridge, MA: Harvard University Press, 1983.

Frum, David. "Ending Illegal Immigration Benefits Economy - CNN.com," May 3, 2010. http://www.cnn.com/2010/OPINION/05/03/frum.immigration.education/index.html.

Fulghum, Robert. *All I Really Need To Know I Learned in Kindergarten*. New York: Ballantine Books, 2004.

Furedi, Frank. *On Tolerance: A Defence of Moral Independence*. London; New York: Continuum, 2011.

Gallagher, Maggie. "Don't Blame Me for Gay Teen Suicides." *New York Post*, October 19, 2010. http://www.nypost.com/p/news/opinion/opedcolumnists/don_blame_me_for_gay_teen_suicides_l1Wt32kEJFFve2SzkjbpYP?CMP.

Ganga, Maria L. La. "Berkeley High May Cut Lab Classes to Fund Programs for Struggling Students." *Los Angeles Times*, January 24, 2010. http://articles.latimes.com/2010/jan/24/local/la-me-berkeley-schools24-2010jan24.

Gavin, Patrick. "Kagan's Journo Friends." *Politico*, May 12, 2010. http://www.politico.com/blogs/onmedia/0510/Kagans_journo_friends.html.

George, Robert P. "'Shameless Acts' Revisited: Some Questions for Martha Nussbaum." *Academic Questions* 9, no. 1 (Winter 1995–1996): 24–42.

Gladwell, Malcolm. *Blink: The Power of Thinking Without Thinking*. New York: Little, Brown and Company, 2005.

Gottfried, Paul Edward. "The Limits of Race." *Taki's Magazine*, May 20, 2009. http://web.archive.org/web/20100701123710/http://www.takimag.com/blogs/article/thinking_about_white_nationalists.

———. *Multiculturalism and the Politics of Guilt: Toward a Secular Theocracy*. University of Missouri Press, 2002.

———. *The Strange Death of Marxism: The European Left in the New Millenium*. University of Missouri Press, 2005.

Graham, Jesse, Brian A. Nosek, and Jonathan Haidt. "The Moral Stereotypes of Liberals and Conservatives: Exaggeration of Differences Across the Political Spectrum." *PLoS ONE* 7, no. 12 (December 12, 2012): e50092. doi:10.1371/journal.pone.0050092.

Green, David G, and John D.G Grieve. *Institutional Racism and the Police?: Fact or Fiction?* London: Institute for the Study of Civil Society, 2000. http://www.civitas.org.uk/pdf/cs06.pdf.

Gross, Paul R., and Norman Levitt. *Higher Superstition: The Academic Left and Its Quarrels with Science*. The Johns Hopkins University Press, 1994.

Grutter v. Bollinger, 539 U.S. 306 (2003).

Guhname, Ron. "Are Attitudes Changing on IQ and Race?" *Inductivist*, May 24, 2008. http://inductivist.blogspot.com/2008/05/are-attitudes-changing-on-iq-and-race.html.

———. "Liberals and Family." *Inductivist*, July 31, 2012. http://inductivist.blogspot.com/2012/07/liberals-and-family.html.

———. "Political Moderation Shrinks as Years of Schooling Grow." *Inductivist*, July 5, 2006. http://inductivist.blogspot.com/2006/07/political-moderation-shrinks-as-years.html.

———. "There Is No Silent but Sensible HBD Majority." *Inductivist*, December 30, 2010. http://inductivist.blogspot.com/2010/12/there-is-no-silent-but-sensible-hbd.html.

Guzzardi, Joe. "What Kind Of Waste Are They Managing?" *VDARE*, May 27, 2003. http://vdare.com/guzzardi/waste_management.htm.

Hacker, Andrew. *Two Nations: Black and White, Separate, Hostile, Unequal.* New York: Scribner, 2003.

Haidt, Jonathan. *The Righteous Mind: Why Good People Are Divided by Politics and Religion.* New York: Pantheon, 2012.

"Hasty Call for Amnesty - New York Times." *New York Times*. Accessed April 30, 2013. http://www.nytimes.com/2000/02/22/opinion/hasty-call-for-amnesty.html.

Health, United States 2011: With Special Feature on Socioeconomic Status and Health. National Center for Health Statistics, May 2012. http://www.cdc.gov/nchs/data/hus/hus11.pdf.

Heartiste. "Chateau Heartiste: Where Pretty Lies Perish.," June 1, 2012. http://heartiste.wordpress.com/.

Heckman, James J., and Brook S. Payner. "Determining the Impact of Federal Antidisrimination Policy on the Economic Status of Blacks: A Study of South Carolina." *American Economic Review* 79 (1989): 138–177.

Hennessey, Matthew. "The Freedom to Homeschool." *First Things - On the Square*, August 17, 2012. http://www.firstthings.com/onthesquare/2012/08/the-freedom-to-homeschool.

Herrnstein, Richard, and Charles Murray. *The Bell Curve: Intelligence and Class Structure in American Life.* New York: Free Press, 1994.

Historical Statistics of the United States, Millennial Edition. Vol. 2. Cambridge University Press, 2006.

Horn, Charisse Van. "Colin Powell Speaks About Racial Profiling and Gates." *Examiner.com*, July 29, 2009. http://www.examiner.com/us-headlines-in-national/colin-powell-speaks-about-racial-profiling-and-gates.

Horowitz, Dr Carl F. *The Authoritarian Roots of Corporate Diversity Training: Jane Elliott's Captive Eyes And Minds.* National Legal and Policy Center, July 2007. http://www.nlpc.org/sites/default/files/CorDiv_SR.pdf.

Hoste, Richard. "Smart People Playing Dumb." *Alternative Right*, April 17, 2010. http://www.alternativeright.com/main/blogs/hbd-human-biodiversity/smart-people-playing-dumb/.

Hunt-Grubbe, Charlotte. "The Elementary DNA of Dr Watson." *The Times*, October 14, 2007.

Hymowitz, Kay S. "The New Girl Order." *City Journal* (Autumn 2007). http://www.city-journal.org/html/17_4_new_girl_order.html.

Income Inequality and Poverty Rising in Most OECD Countries, October 21, 2008. http://www.oecd.org/general/incomeinequalityandpovertyrisinginmostoecdcountries.htm.

Jaeger, Werner. *Paideia: The Ideals of Greek Culture*. Volume III: The Conflict of Cultural Ideals in the Age of Plato. Oxford University Press, 1986.

Jan, Tracy. "E-mail on Race Sparks a Furor at Harvard Law: Student Regrets Questioning the Intelligence of Blacks." *Boston Globe*, April 30, 2010. http://www.boston.com/news/local/massachusetts/articles/2010/04/30/e_mail_on_race_sparks_a_furor_at_harvard_law/.

Jensen, Arthur R. *The g Factor: The Science of Mental Ability*. Westport, CT: Praeger, 1998.

Jensen, Kristin. "Obama Tops Romney in Poll With 2-1 Backing From Single Women." *Bloomberg*. Accessed January 31, 2013. http://www.bloomberg.com/news/2012-07-11/obama-tops-romney-in-poll-with-2-1-backing-from-single-women.html.

Jeory, Ted. "Why Try to Take Baby From EDL Mother but Not From 'Terrorists'?" *Sunday Express*, June 17, 2012. http://www.express.co.uk/posts/view/327086/Why-try-to-take-baby-from-EDL-mother-but-not-from-terrorists.

Johnson, K.C. "Baker: In His Own Words." *Durham-in-Wonderland*, January 1, 2007. http://durhamwonderland.blogspot.com/2007/01/baker-in-his-own-words.html.

Jones, Leigh. "WORLD | Appeals Court Denies Homeschooling Family's Asylum Claim." *WORLD*, May 14, 2013. http://www.worldmag.com/2013/05/appeals_court_denies_homeschooling_family_s_asylum_claim.

Jones, Stanton L. "Sexual Orientation and Reason: On the Implications of False Beliefs About Homosexuality." *Center for Applied Christian Ethics*, January 2012. http://www.wheaton.edu/CACE/Hot-Topics.

Jussim, Lee. *Social Perception and Social Reality: Why Accuracy Dominates Bias and Self-Fulfilling Prophecy*. Oxford University Press, USA, 2012.

Jussim, Lee J., Clark R. McCauley, and Yueh-Ting Lee, eds. *Stereotype Accuracy: Toward Appreciating Group Differences*. American Psychological Association, 1995.

Kalb, James. "After Liberalism: Notes Toward Reconstruction." *The Intercollegiate Review* 47, no. 1 (Spring 2012): 23–31.

———. *The Tyranny of Liberalism: Understanding and Overcoming Administered Freedom, Inquisitorial Tolerance, and Equality by Command*. Wilmington, DE: ISI Books, 2008.

Kaufmann, Eric. *Shall the Religious Inherit the Earth?: Demography and Politics in the Twenty-First Century*. London: Profile Books, 2011.

Kern, Soeren. *A Black Day for Austria*. Gatestone Institute, December

26, 2011. http://www.gatestoneinstitute.org/2702/sabaditsch-wolf
f-appeal.

Kochhar, Rakesh, Richard Fry, and Paul Taylor. *Wealth Gaps Rise to Record Highs Between Whites, Blacks, Hispanics.* Pew Research Center, July 26, 2011. http://www.pewsocialtrends.org/2011/07/26/wealth-gaps-rise-to-record-highs-between-whites-blacks-hispanics.

Konrath, Sara H, Edward H O'Brien, and Courtney Hsing. "Changes in Dispositional Empathy in American College Students over Time: a Meta-analysis." *Personality and Social Psychology Review: An Official Journal of the Society for Personality and Social Psychology, Inc* 15, no. 2 (May 2011): 180–198. doi:10.1177/1088868310377395.

Lander, Christian. *Stuff White People Like: A Definitive Guide to the Unique Taste of Millions.* New York: Random House Trade Paperbacks, 2008.

Layton, Lyndsey. "ACLU Alleges Michigan School District Violated Students' 'Right to Learn to Read'." *Washington Post* (July 12, 2012).

Lazartigues, A., P. Planche, S. Saint-André, and H. Morales. "New society, new families: a new basic personality? From the neurotic to the narcissistic-hedonistic personality." *Encephale* 33, no. 3 Pt 1 (June 2007): 293–9.

"Legal Clips >> NAACP's Federal Complaint Claims Entrance Exam for New York City's Elite Schools Is Racially Discriminatory." Accessed January 11, 2013. http://legalclips.nsba.org/?p=16490.

Levin, Yuval. "Science and the Left." *The New Atlantis* no. 19 (Winter 2008): 15–34.

Lipton, Eric, and Eric Lichtblau. "In Black Caucus, a Fund-Raising Powerhouse." *The New York Times*, February 14, 2010, sec. U.S. / Politics. http://www.nytimes.com/2010/02/14/us/politics/14cbc.html.

Longman, Phillip. "The Global Baby Bust." *Foreign Affairs* 83, no. 3 (June 2004): 64–79.

Lynch, Frederic. *Invisible Victims: White Males and the Crisis of Affirmative Action.* Westport, CT: Praeger, 1991.

Mac Donald, Heather. "Elites to Anti-Affirmative-Action Voters: Drop Dead." *City Journal* (Winter 2007). http://www.city-journal.org/html/17_1_prop209.html.

———. "Harvard's Faustian Bargain." *City Journal*, February 2007.

———. "Is the Criminal-Justice System Racist?" *City Journal*, Spring 2008. http://www.city-journal.org/2008/18_2_criminal_justice_system.html.

MailOnline. "Christian Preacher on Hooligan Charge after Saying He Believes That Homosexuality Is a Sin," May 1, 2010. http://www.dailymail.co.uk/news/article-1270364/Christian-preacher-hooligan-charge-saying-believes-homosexuality-sin.html.

Malcolm, Andrew. "Oh-oh! Politicians Share Personality Traits with Serial Killers: Study." *Top of the Ticket - Los Angeles Times*, June 15, 2009. http://latimesblogs.latimes.com/washington/2009/06/politicians-and-serial-killers.html.

Mandelbaum, Robb. "U.S. Push on Illegal Bias Against Hiring Those With Criminal Records." *The New York Times* (June 21, 2012): B8.

Mangan, Dennis. "The Persecution of Politically Incorrect Scientists." *Alternative Right*, April 28, 2010. http://www.alternativeright.com/main/blogs/hbd-human-biodiversity/the-persecution-of-politically-incorrect-scientists/.

Marks, Loren. "Same-sex Parenting and Children's Outcomes: A Closer Examination of the American Psychological Association's Brief on Lesbian and Gay Parenting." *Social Science Research* 41, no. 4 (July 2012): 735–751. doi:10.1016/j.ssresearch.2012.03.006.

McGowan, William. *Coloring the News: How Crusading for Diversity Has Corrupted American Journalism*. San Francisco: Encounter Books, 2001.

"Merriam-Webster.com," October 11, 2011. http://www.merriam-webster.com/dictionary/.

Messner, Thomas M. *The Price of Prop 8*. Backgrounder. Heritage Foundation, October 22, 2009. http://s3.amazonaws.com/thf_media/2009/pdf/bg2328.pdf.

Milgram, Stanley. *Obedience to Authority: an Experimental View*. New York: Harper, 2009.

Miller, Edward M. "The Relevance of Group Membership for Personnel Selection: A Demonstration Using Bayes' Theorem." *The Journal of Social, Political, and Economic Studies* 19, no. 3 (Fall 1994): 323–359.

Mooney, Chris. *The Republican War on Science*. New York: Basic Books, 2005.

Morgenson, Gretchen, and Joshua Rosner. *Reckless Endangerment: How Outsized Ambition, Greed, and Corruption Led to Economic Armageddon*. New York: Times Books, 2011.

Mullarkey, Maureen. "Freedom of Speech—Unless You Annoy the Wrong People." *Weekly Standard*, March 16, 2010. http://www.weeklystandard.com/Content/Public/Articles/000/000/016/252zsbwa.asp.

Munro, Neil. "Slotting Scientists: Higher-education Officials Are Trying to Boost Diversity in Science Departments Without Running Afoul of the Supreme Court." *National Journal*, December 19, 2009. http://conventions.nationaljournal.com/njmagazine/id_20091219_2170.php.

Murray, Charles. *Coming Apart: The State of White America, 1960–2010*. New York: Crown Forum, 2012.

———. *Human Accomplishment: The Pursuit of Excellence in the Arts and Sciences, 800 BC to 1950*. New York: HarperCollins, 2003.

Noonan, Peggy. "Failures of Imagination." *The Wall Street Journal*, June 21, 2002.

"Nov. 8: Casey, Barbour, Rendell, Roundtable, Brokaw - Meet the Press | NBC News." *"Meet the Press" Transcript*. Accessed January

10, 2013. http://www.msnbc.msn.com/id/33752275/ns/meet_the_press/#.UO8Nh6zaS8o.

Obama, Barack. "Executive Order—White House Initiative on Educational Excellence for African Americans." The White House Office of the Press Secretary, July 26, 2012. http://www.whitehouse.gov/the-press-office/2012/07/26/executive-order-white-house-initiative-educational-excellence-african-am.

"Online Etymology Dictionary: Definition of 'Speculation.'" Online Etymology Dictionary. Accessed January 31, 2013. http://www.etymonline.com/index.php?term=speculation.

Otterman, Sharon. "Diversity Debate Engulfs Hunter High in Manhattan." The New York Times, August 4, 2010, sec. N.Y. / Region. http://www.nytimes.com/2010/08/05/nyregion/05hunter.html.

Panné, Jean-Louis, Andrzej Paczkowski, Karel Bartosek, Jean-Louis Margolin, Nicolas Werth, and Stéphane Courtois. The Black Book of Communism: Crimes, Terror, Repression. Edited by Mark Kramer. Translated by Mark Kramer and Jonathan Murphy. Harvard University Press, 1999.

Partner, Steve. "Is Angling a Racist Sport?", September 10, 2010. http://www.gofishing.co.uk/Angling-Times/Section/News--Catches/General-News/September-2010/Steve-Partner-Is-angling-a-racist-sport/.

Pinker, Steven. The Blank Slate: The Modern Denial of Human Nature. New York: Viking, 2002.

Planned Parenthood of Southeastern Pa. v. Casey, 505 U.S. 833 (1992).

Pollan, Michael. "Against Nativism." The New York Times Magazine, May 15, 1994. http://michaelpollan.com/articles-archive/against-nativism/.

Pope Benedict XVI. "Angelus." December 24, 2006. http://www.vatican.va/holy_father/benedict_xvi/angelus/2006/documents/hf_ben-xvi_ang_20061224_en.html.

Pope John Paul II. "Apostolic Exhortation Familiaris Consortio," November 22, 1981. http://www.vatican.va/holy_father/john_paul_ii/apost_exhortations/documents/hf_jp-ii_exh_19811122_familiaris-consortio_en.html.

———. "Apostolic Letter Dilecti Amici of Pope John Paul II to the Youth of the World on the Occasion of International Youth Year," March 31, 1985. http://www.vatican.va/holy_father/john_paul_ii/apost_letters/documents/hf_jp-ii_apl_31031985_dilecti-amici_en.html.

———. "Apostolos Suos," May 21, 1998. http://www.vatican.va/holy_father/john_paul_ii/motu_proprio/documents/hf_jp-ii_motu-proprio_22071998_apostolos-suos_en.html.

———. "Centesimus Annus," May 1, 1991. http://www.vatican.va/holy_father/john_paul_ii/encyclicals/documents/hf_jp-ii_enc_01051991_centesimus-annus_en.html.

———. "Evangelium Vitae," March 25, 1995. http://www.vatican.va/

holy_father/john_paul_ii/encyclicals/documents/hf_jp-
ii_enc_25031995_evangelium-vitae_en.html.

———. "Message of the Holy Father John Paul II for the 89th World
Day of Migrants and Refugees," October 24, 2002. http://
www.vatican.va/holy_father/john_paul_ii/messages/migration/
documents/hf_jp-ii_mes_20021202_world-migration-day-
2003_en.html.

Pope Pius XI. "Mit Brennender Sorge," March 14, 1937. http://
www.vatican.va/holy_father/pius_xi/encyclicals/documents/
hf_p-xi_enc_14031937_mit-brennender-sorge_en.html.

Prince, Rosa. "Gordon Brown Calls Campaigner 'Bigoted Woman.'"
The Telegraph, April 28, 2010, sec. election-2010. http://www.tele-
graph.co.uk/news/election-2010/7645072/Gordon-Brown-calls-
campaigner-bigoted-woman.html.

Protecting the Force: Lessons from Fort Hood. Department of Defense, January 10, 2010. http://www.defense.gov/pubs/pdfs/DOD-Protec-
tingTheForce-Web_Security_HR_13jan10.pdf.

Putnam, Robert D. "E Pluribus Unum: Diversity and Community in
the Twenty-first Century." *Scandinavian Political Studies* 30, no. 2
(June 2007): 137–174.

Rawls, John. *Political Liberalism*. Columbia University Press, 1993.

Regnerus, Mark. "How Different Are the Adult Children of Parents
Who Have Same-sex Relationships? Findings from the New Family Structures Study." *Social Science Journal* 41 (2012): 752–770.

Reilly, Robert R. *The Closing of the Muslim Mind: How Intellectual Suicide
Created the Modern Islamist*. Wilmington, DE: ISI Books, 2010.

Reisman, Judith A. "Crafting Bi/Homosexual Youth." *Regent University Law Review* 14 (2002): 283–342.

Reisman, Judith A., and Edward W. Eichel. *Kinsey, Sex and Fraud: The
Indoctrination of a People*. Lafayette, LA: Lochinvar-Huntington
House, 1990.

Ricci v. DeStefano, 129 S. Ct. 2658 (2009).

Rimer, Sara, and Karen W. Arenson. "Top Colleges Take More
Blacks, but Which Ones?" *The New York Times* (June 24, 2004).

Romer v. Evans, 517 U.S. 620 (1996).

Rosenberg, Alex. "The Disenchanted Naturalist's Guide to Reality."
On the Human, November 9, 2009. http://onthehuman.org/2009/
11/the-disenchanted-naturalists-guide-to-reality/.

Rubenstein, Edwin S., and the NPI staff. *Affirmative Action and the Economic Costs of "Diversity."* Research and Assessment from the National Policy Institute 803. The National Policy Institute, 2008.

Rushton, J. Philippe. *Race, Evolution, and Behavior: A Life History Perspective*. 3rd ed. Port Huron, MI: Charles Darwin Research Institute
Press, 2000.

Saad, Lydia. *Tea Partiers Are Fairly Mainstream in Their Demographics*.
Gallup, April 5, 2010. http://www.gallup.com/poll/127181/Tea-
Partiers-Fairly-Mainstream-Demographics.aspx?utm_source=aler

t&utm_medium=email&utm_campaign=syndication&utm_con
tent=morelink&utm_term=Politics.

Sacks, David O., and Peter A. Thiel. *The Diversity Myth: Multiculturalism and Political Intolerance on Campus.* Oakland, CA: The Independent Institute, 1998.

Sailer, Steve. "Countrywide's Angelo Mozilo: He Warned Us—But
Washington Didn't Want To Know." *VDARE,* June 22, 2009. http://
/www.vdare.com/node/11997.

———. "Test Case." *The American Conservative,* September 10, 2007. http://isteve.blogspot.com/2007/11/steve-sailers-test-case_4916.ht-
ml.

———. "The Diversity Recession." *Taki's Magazine,* June 22, 2008. http://takimag.com/article/the_diversity_recession2#axzz1ajbSC6
Qj.

———. "The Minority Mortgage Meltdown: More Evidence—But
Our Elite Doesn't Want To Know." *VDARE,* June 20, 2010. http://
vdare.com/sailer/100620_mortgage_meltdown.htm.

———. "Why Multicultural Societies Are Less Creative." *iSteve,* May
15, 2006. http://isteve.blogspot.com/2006/05/why-multicultural-
societies-are-less.html.

Salingaros, Nikos A. "The Derrida Virus." *Telos* no. 126 (winter 2003):
66–82.

———. *Anti-Architecture and Deconstruction.* Third Edition. Solingen,
Germany: Umbau-Verlag, 2008.

Salter, Jim. "Professor Dumped from Oil Spill Team over Writings."
Boston.com, May 19, 2010. http://www.boston.com/news/educa-
tion/higher/articles/2010/05/19/professor_dumped_from_oil_sp
ill_team_over_writings/.

Sander, Richard H. "A Systemic Analysis of Affirmative Action in
American Law Schools." *Stanford Law Review* 57 (November 2004):
367–483.

Sartre, Jean-Paul. *Anti-Semite and Jew.* New York: Schocken, 1995.

Saul, John Ralston. *Reflections of a Siamese Twin: Canada at the End of the
Twentieth Century.* Toronto: Viking, 1997.

Savill, Richard. "Preacher's Conviction over Anti-gay Sign Upheld."
Telegraph.co.uk, January 14, 2004, sec. uknews. http://www. tele-
graph.co.uk/news/uknews/1451593/Preachers-conviction-over-an
ti-gay-sign-upheld.html.

Schmidt, Peter. "Investigators Say Naval Academy Punished Professor
Who Criticized Affirmative Action." *The Chronicle of Higher Education,* January 26, 2011.

Schwartz, Howard S. "The Clash of Moralities in the Program of Diversity," October 10, 2011. http://www.sba.oakland.edu/faculty/
schwartz/Clash%20of%20moralities.htm.

Scinto, Madeleine. "Randy Grands Take over Online Realm - Number
of Seniors Playing the Field More Than Doubles." *New York Post,*
February 26, 2013. http://www.nypost.com/p/news/national/

randy_grands_doubles_over_online_IEObiiAdWcmEM4sLnIUiY
N.

Scruton, Roger. "Why I Became a Conservative." *The New Criterion*,
February 2003. http://archive.frontpagemag.com/readArticle.as-
px?ARTID=19900.

Second Vatican Council. "Pastoral Constitution on the Church in the
Modern World," December 7, 1965. http://www.vatican.va/ar-
chive/hist_councils/ii_vatican_council/documents/vat-ii_cons_i
9651207_gaudium-et-spes_en.html.

Serwer, Adam. "How to Profile a Terrorist." *The American Prospect*,
September 23, 2010. http://www.prospect.org/csnc/blogs/adam_
serwer_archive?month=09&year=2010&base_name=how_to_pr
ofile_a_terrorist.

Siegel, Lee. "What's Race Got to Do With It?" *Campaign Stops*, January 14, 2012. http://campaignstops.blogs.nytimes.com/2012/01/
14/whats-race-got-to-do-with-it/.

Smith, Christian. "An Academic Auto-da-Fé." *The Chronicle of Higher
Education*, July 23, 2012, sec. The Chronicle Review. http://chroni-
cle.com/article/article-content/133107/.

Smith, Christian, Kari Christoffersen, Hilary Davidson, and Patricia
Snell Herzog. *Lost in Transition: The Dark Side of Emerging Adulthood*. Oxford University Press, 2011.

Sokal, Alan, and Jean Bricmont. *Fashionable Nonsense: Postmodern Intellectuals' Abuse of Science*. New York: Picador, 1999.

Sowell, Thomas. *Civil Rights: Rhetoric or Reality?* New York: W. Mor-
row, 1984.

Spencer, Robert. "Army Ignored Warning Signs from Fort Hood Jihadist Because It 'Valued the Diversity of Having a Muslim Psychiatrist'." *Jihad Watch*, February 22, 2010. http://www.jihadwatch.
org/2010/02/army-ignored-warning-signs-from-fort-hood-jihadist-
because-it-valued-the-diversity-of-having-a-musli.html.

Stalin, Joseph. "Reply to an Inquiry of the Jewish News Agency in the
United States." In *Works*, 13: July 1930–January 1934: 30. Moscow:
Foreign Languages Publishing House, 1954.

"STDs Running Rampant In Retirement Community: Doctor Blames
Viagra, Lack Of Sex Education." *Click Orlando*, May 27, 2006. http://
/www.clickorlando.com/news/9283707/detail.html.

Stevenson, Betsey, and Justin Wolfers. "The Paradox of Declining Female Happiness." *American Economic Journal: Economic Policy* 1, no.
2 (July 2009): 190–225. doi:10.1257/pol.1.2.190.

Street, Paul. "Race, Prison, and Poverty: The Race to Incarcerate in
the Age of Correctional Keynesianism." *Z Magazine* (May 2001): 27.

Summers, Lawrence H. "Remarks at NBER Conference on Diversifying the Science & Engineering Workforce." Harvard University
Office of the President, January 14, 2005. http://web.archive.org/
web/20080130023006/http://www.president.harvard.edu/speech-
es/2005/nber.html.

"Swedish Politician Calls for Even Harsher Penalties for Homeschooling." *LifeSite*, January 17, 2012. http://www.lifesitenews.com/news/swedish-politician-leader-calls-for-even-harsher-penalties-for-homeschoolin.

Tavernise, Sabrina. "Life Expectancy for Less Educated Whites in U.S. Is Shrinking." *The New York Times*, September 20, 2012, sec. U.S. http://www.nytimes.com/2012/09/21/us/life-expectancy-for-less-educated-whites-in-us-is-shrinking.html.

Taylor, Jared. *Paved with Good Intentions: The Failure of Race Relations in Contemporary America*. New York: Carroll & Graf, 1993.

Taylor, Stuart. "Why Feminist Careerists Neutered Larry Summers." *The Atlantic*, February 2005.

Telles, Edward E., and Vilma Ortiz. *Generations of Exclusion: Mexican Americans, Assimilation, and Race*. New York: Russell Sage Foundation, 2008.

The Color of Crime: Race, Crime and Justice in America. Second, Expanded Edition. Oakton, VA: New Century Foundation, 2005. http://www.colorofcrime.com/colorofcrime2005.pdf.

Thernstrom, Abigail, and Stephan Thernstrom. "Black Progress: How Far We've Come, and How Far We Have to Go." *The Brookings Institution*, Spring 1998. http://www.brookings.edu/research/articles/1998/03/spring-affirmativeaction-thernstrom.

Thernstrom, Stephan. "The Scandal of the Law Schools." *Commentary*, December 1997.

Thompson, Krissah, and Dan Balz. "Rand Paul Comments About Civil Rights Stir Controversy." *The Washington Post*, May 21, 2010, sec. Politics. http://www.washingtonpost.com/wp-dyn/content/article/2010/05/20/AR2010052003500.html.

Thompson, Mark. "The Fort Hood Report: Why No Mention of Islam?" *Time*, January 20, 2010. http://www.time.com/time/nation/article/0,8599,1954960,00.html.

Tilove, Jonathan. "The Gap: In a Single Statistic, the Measure of a Racial Tragedy." *Jonathan Tilove*, May 5, 2005. http://jonathantilove.com/black-men-missing/.

Twenge, Jean M. *Generation Me: Why Today's Young Americans Are More Confident, Assertive, Entitled–and More Miserable Than Ever Before*. New York: Free Press, 2007.

Twenge, Jean M., Elise C. Freeman, and W. Keith Campbell. "Generational Differences in Young Adults' Life Goals, Concern for Others, and Civic Orientation, 1966–2009." *Journal of Personality and Social Psychology* 102, no. 5 (n.d.): 1045–1062. Accessed January 29, 2013.

"Uniform Guidelines on Employee Selection Procedures (1978)." Federal Government, August 25, 1978. http://uniformguidelines.com/uniformguidelines.html.

Unz, Ron. "The Myth of American Meritocracy." *The American Conservative*, November 28, 2012. http://www.theamericanconservative.com/articles/the-myth-of-american-meritocracy/.

"Urban Dictionary: Definition of 'Tea Bagger'." *Urban Dictionary*, October 13, 2011. http://www.urbandictionary.com/define.php?te rm=tea%20bagger.

USCCR. *The Educational Effectiveness of Historically Black College and Universities.* United States Commission on Civil Rights, 2010.

Wade, Nicholas. "Study Debunks Stephen Jay Gould's Claim of Racism on Morton Skulls." *The New York Times*, June 13, 2011, sec. Science. http://www.nytimes.com/2011/06/14/science/14skull.html.

Waite, Linda J., and Maggie Gallagher. *The Case for Marriage: Why Married People Are Happier, Healthier, and Better Off Financially.* New York: Doubleday, 2000.

Waldron, Jeremy. *The Harm in Hate Speech (Oliver Wendell Holmes Lectures, 2009).* Harvard University Press, 2012.

Wax, Amy. *Race, Wrongs, and Remedies: Group Justice in the 21st Century.* Lanham, MD: Rowman and Littlefield Publishers, 2009.

———. "The Dead End of 'Disparate Impact'." *National Affairs*, Summer 2012. http://www.nationalaffairs.com/publications/detail/ the-dead-end-of-disparate-impact.

Weisbuch, Max, Kristin Pauker, and Nalini Ambady. "The Subtle Transmission of Race Bias via Televised Nonverbal Behavior." *Science* 326, no. 5960 (December 18, 2009): 1711–1714. doi:10.1126/science.1178358.

Weissberg, Robert. "The Siren Song of Diversity," March 1, 2010. http://www.alternativeright.com/main/the-magazine/the-siren-song-of-diversity/.

———. "The Stealthy War on Smart Kids." *Mensa Research Journal* 40, no. 2 (Summer 2009): 14–21.

Wheeler, Brian. "EU States 'Must Be Multicultural'," June 21, 2012, sec. UK Politics. http://www.bbc.co.uk/news/uk-politics-1851 9395.

Whittle, Peter. "Muzzled Britain." *City Journal*, Winter 2013. http://www.city-journal.org/2013/eon0109pw.html.

Will, George. "Time for Bush to See the Realities of Iraq." *Washington Post* (May 4, 2004): A25.

Williams, Walter. "Gender-Norming Update." *Capitalism Magazine*, April 4, 1997. http://capitalismmagazine.com/1997/04/gender-no rming-update/.

Williamson, Chilton, Jr. "A Practicing Catholic Considers Why 'The Church' Is Wrong About Immigration." *VDARE*, April 22, 2008. http://vdare.com/williamson/080422_immigration.htm.

Wood, Peter. *Diversity: The Invention of a Concept.* San Francisco: Encounter Books, 2003.

Yamagishi, Toshio, and Nobuhiro Mifune. "Social Exchange and Solidarity: In-group Love or Out-group Hate?" *Evolution and Human Behavior* 30, no. 4 (July 2009): 229–237. doi:10.1016/j.evolhumbehav.2009.02.004.

Bibliography

Yap, Stevie C.Y., Ivana Anusic, and Richard E. Lucas. "Does Personality Moderate Reaction and Adaptation to Major Life Events? Evidence from the British Household Panel Survey." *Journal of Research in Personality* 46, no. 5 (October 2012): 477–488. doi:10.1016/j.jrp.2012.05.005.

Made in the USA
Lexington, KY
09 March 2014